MW00929277

God Delights in the
Prayers of His Children

Finish the race
God bless
Terri Flynn

God Delights in the Prayers of His Children

Praying God's Word Back to Him through Scripture-Based Prayers

Terri Flynn

iUniverse LLC
Bloomington

God Delights in the Prayers of His Children
Praying God's Word Back to Him through Scripture-Based Prayers

iUniverse books may be ordered through booksellers or by contacting:

iUniverse LLC
1663 Liberty Drive
Bloomington, IN 47403
www.iuniverse.com
1-800-Authors (1-800-288-4677)

ISBN: 978-1-4759-7150-7 (sc)
ISBN: 978-1-4759-7151-4 (hc)
ISBN: 978-1-4759-7152-1 (ebk)

Library of Congress Control Number: 2013901113

Printed in the United States of America

iUniverse rev. date: 03/06/2013

Dedication

I would like to extend my gratitude to my family and church.

To my husband, Sean, thank you for being my helper, my best friend, my prayer partner, the love of my life, and so much more. I am grateful that God gives us second chances. You are my yes and amen.

To my son, Danny, thank you for encouraging and believing in me.

To Jennifer, Hannah, Jodi, Jack, Mary, and Molly, I didn't give you the gift of life; life gave me the gift of you.

To my niece Rachael, thank you for convincing me to complete this book. You are a blessing to me.

To my church, Free Chapel Worship Center, and my pastor, Jentezen Franklin, thank you for speaking God's truths. My heart—and my life—are changed forever.

This book is an outcome of countless prayers that I have prayed for all of you. I love you all with all my heart, and you are always in my prayers.

Contents

Preface

Dear Reader,

This book began as part of my Christian walk. In 2000, I started writing down my prayers as I began searching the Scriptures to see what the Bible said about the struggles and challenges I was experiencing. I discovered that praying with Scriptures for understanding, wisdom, and intimacy with God developed my faith, character, and spiritual growth.

Nearly a decade after that first written prayer, I started compiling *God Delights in the Prayers of His Children.* I fashioned this book from personal needs, experiences, and desires, and consequently, I have written many prayers for children, loved ones, finances, and even for myself.

As you read this book, you will learn about how Scripture clearly encourages us to go to God with our requests, and we are to do so with a spirit of gratitude. The thought of God's all powerful might in my situation has inspired me to pray with Scripture. God does not discourage us from approaching Him with our needs, desires, and dreams. Just the opposite! He wants us to talk to Him about everything. God is generous to His children, and when we request things that are in His will, God promises to grant them. We can knock on the door of heaven with faith, and confidence, and enter His throne with self-assurance, and certainty that we are heirs with Christ Jesus.

So what qualifications do I have to write this book? My qualifications and inspiration come from my passion to experience an intimate relationship with God and to receive answers to my prayers. For over a decade, I have directly experienced the power of praying with

Scriptures, and I have truly seen miraculous answers to my prayers by praying God's Word back to Him.

This book has been prepared to assist those who are seeking God in prayer. So often we may not be sure what to pray for. However, we can count on the Holy Spirit. He knows all about God's Word and all about our needs. Each day, we need to ask God by praying and reading His Word to show us how to bring His Word and our prayers together. After all, being in the perfect will of God and living according to His revealed will should be the highest aspiration of our lives.

There are many prayer books on the market already. Why yet another book? Here are some of the reasons that distinguish this book from others currently available on the market:

- This prayer book offers creative ideas to get you started in prayer.
- These inspirational prayers will motivate you too make prayer a daily part of your life.
- Each section includes prayers for specific people and their needs.
- You'll find prayers that consist of Scriptures dealing with particular situations.
- It will encourage you to develop an intimate relationship with God by praying His Word back to Him.

These are a few reasons you will find this book valuable.

Praying with the Bible provides the practical help and insight we all need so that we can pray more consistently and effectively. Praying this way fills us with fresh understanding of God's Word and creates faith-building confidence that God will do all He said He will do. Praying with Scriptures will increase your spiritual growth, and you will discover what God says about certain situations. The Bible is our instruction manual for life, and by praying God's Word back to Him, we show Him we agree with Him.

Using this Prayer Book

The goal of this book is not just to emphasis the importance of prayer, but to help your prayer life to grow more fruitful by suggesting ways to incorporate Scripture into your everyday prayers. God Delights in the Prayer of His Children provides Scripture-based prayers for all kinds of life's situations; from honoring God, to praying for children, loved ones, finances, and even yourself. As you meditate on the Scriptures woven into these prayers, allow them to enter your heart, and speak them out loud. Use these prayers in addition to, not instead of, your personal prayers to God.

This book is comprised of six chapters. Chapter one provides information about the importance of prayer and offers suggestions on how to build a stronger prayer life. It also includes Scriptures that reveal why God commands us to pray.

Chapters two through six include prayers focused around a specific topic. Each of these chapters follows a similar pattern, and consists of three sections.

> Section 1, provides an explanation on why it is important to pray for the area covered in that chapter.
>
> Section 2, contains a list of Scriptures which identify the promises that God has already made on the subject.
>
> Section 3, presents prayers focused upon and based on God's word. These prayers will cover a variety of life's circumstances and pertain to the focus of that chapter. The end of each prayer also includes the key Scripture that was highlighted in that specific prayer.

If you would like to pray for a particular person or purpose; please feel free to personalize any of these prayers. You can always replace the words children; loved ones, son, daughter, etc., with the names or purpose needed to personalize it.

I hope that reading this book points you to the Word of God; deepens your understanding of His promises to you and for you; and that these prayers will provide assistance in your journey to a more intimate relationship with Him.

CHAPTER 1

How to Grow Closer to God

Establishing a Prayer Life

Prayer brings about nourishment and growth to your spirit. Think of prayer as breathing. Just as breathing is essential to your physical life, your prayer life is essential to your spiritual life. Breathing consists of both inhaling and exhaling. Your prayers should consist of talking to God and then listening and receiving from God. Too often our prayers get reduced to simply asking God for things. Since praying is a conversation between you and God, this conversation, like one in any healthy relationship, should be about more than just asking.

Take some time to praise God and spend time in worship. Ask for forgiveness and repent to God daily for the things you have done wrong. Surrender your thoughts, your words, and your actions.

Then ask Him for the things that you need and pray for the needs of other people. Bring your petitions before God and make your requests known to Him. Just as a child asks a parent for what they need, it is all right to ask God for things, because He is your heavenly Father.

Then yield to God and give Him your hopes, your dreams, and your future. Make a commitment that prayer will become a constant part of your daily life. Don't forget to sit and listen. Just sit in silence for a while before the throne of God.

"So I tell you to ask, and you will receive. Search and you will find. Knock and the door will be opened for you. Everyone who asks will receive.

The one who searches will find, and for the person who knocks, the door will be opened." (Luke 11:9-10 GW)

"Never stop praying." (1 Thessalonians 5:17 NLT)

"He says, 'Be still, and know that I am God; I will be exalted among the nations, I will be exalted in the earth." (Psalm 46:10 NIV)

Four Building Blocks of Prayer

All prayer should lead us to a deeper relationship with God. We can pray in secret, with our loved ones, with our church, at any place and at anytime. While there are many ways to pray, I have highlighted four basic building blocks of prayer.

In order to help us recall the important parts of prayer, the acronym ACTS has been developed. This is a simple tool to help us remember the four building blocks of prayer: adoration, confession, thanksgiving, and supplication.

Prayer is just talking with God, but it is an extremely important part of developing and maintaining an intimate relationship with God and growing in Christ. Prayer could be considered the very life breath of true Christianity. To pray effectively, we should regularly include these four building blocks of prayer.

Adoration is the part of prayer where we focus on God. When we start our prayers, we should begin with adoring God and praising Him for who He is. Praise and adoration should arise in a heart full of love toward God. Even Jesus taught us to first love God with all our heart, mind, and soul. Our adoration for God should be done continuously, and it should become as normal to us as breathing.

"Through Jesus, therefore, let us continually offer to God a sacrifice of praise, the fruit of lips that openly profess His name." (Hebrews 13:15 NIV)

Confession of sin is important to our intimate relationship with God. God requires confession of sin as the path that allows us to express our yielded and surrendered hearts to His sovereign will. Only when we acknowledge our offenses toward God can our relationship with God be restored. The Holy Spirit is said to be grieved, and His work quenched by our sin; however, restoration begins when we confess our sins.

"If we confess our sins, he is faithful and just and will forgive us our sins and purify us from all unrighteousness." (1 John 1:9 NIV)

Thanksgiving is thanking God for everything that He is doing for us and for all the amazing things that God has entrusted us with—the most important one being eternal life, which was given to us through the sacrifice of Christ. We cannot be strong and established in our faith without an attitude of gratitude, so don't wait for some special blessing before giving thanks. The breath we are taking right now is a blessing enough. Use it to give thanks. Give thanks for all the blessings of life. Give thanks for food, clothes, family, friends and most of all grace.

"Give praise to the LORD, proclaim his name; make known among the nations what he has done." (1 Chronicles 16:8 NIV)

Supplication is another way of showing faith. In prayers of supplication, we present God with our requests from our hearts, our needs, and our desires. In Revelation 5:8, the prayer bowls seem to play a role in releasing God's power here on earth. The bowls are filled with the prayers of the saints, but the bowls must be full before they are tipped to release God's power. So continue to ask with sincerity, but most of all, ask with faith. Have faith that your heavenly Father is always acting in your best interests, no matter how things may appear.

"When the lamb had taken the scroll, the four living creatures and the 24 leaders bowed in front of him. Each held a harp and a gold bowl full of incense, the prayers of God's holy people." (Revelation 5:8 GWT)

Interceding with Power

The power of the Word of God is unstoppable. The first thing each and every Christian must fully realize is that the Holy Bible is truly the inspired and infallible Word of God. The Word of God is described as a double-edged sword. It is our spiritual weapon of great power, a sword that cuts straight to the heart. It cuts past our excuses and defenses and confronts us with its truth. The sword of the Spirit is powerful and victorious, capable of piercing even the most stubborn mental and spiritual strong-holds with its simple truth. When we are armed with God's Word, we have no need of any other weapons.

Our Christian life is an ongoing spiritual battle between the Spirit of God and the enticement of the Devil. However, we can overcome in our battles by equipping ourselves with God's Word and living a life in agreement with Him. We can have faith and expect God to keep His promises. We can be assured that His Word shall accomplish what He pleases and that His Word shall prosper where He sends it. We will see victory when we choose to believe and speak God's Word.

"For the word of God is alive and active. Sharper than any double-edged sword, it penetrates even to dividing soul and spirit, joints and marrow; it judges the thoughts and attitudes of the heart." (Hebrews 4:12 NIV)

When I hear others pray for me, it brings me hope and courage. It reminds me of the truth of God's Word. We are called to be intercessors because we cannot win this battle alone. We need to become committed intercessors to lift each other up in fervent, specific prayer. Imagine how the power of God might be released in our lives and in this world if we would just pray Scriptures over each other. I am so thankful for the prayers of the body of Christ. I have faith that we are having an impact for the kingdom of God.

"With this in mind, we constantly pray for you, that our God may make you worthy of his calling, and that by his power he may bring to fruition your every desire for goodness and your every deed prompted by faith." (2 Thessalonians 1:11 NIV)

Finding Comfort in God

Comfort can be an uncertain thing if we don't know where to look. We can only find comfort by understanding the difference between what is temporary and what is eternal. When people who have been through difficult circumstances trust in Jesus, they emerge with amazing abilities to be sensitive towards others and to depend on God. That is why we need to fix our eyes on the future hope we have in the unseen parts of life. Jesus promises us that His teachings are true and that God will provide for us now and in eternity.

We can have confidence that God is the God of all comfort and compassion. He notices when we are heartbroken and discouraged and gives us strength and hope so that we can hold our heads up high again. He comforts us during times of trouble so we can comfort others with the comfort that we ourselves have received from Him. As a Christian, we have the promise that the Holy Spirit is our comforter and counselor and that He is called to our side to assist in hardship and sorrow. The Holy Spirit stands by us to help, strengthen, comfort, and eases our loneliness, fear, and grief.

"But the Helper, the Holy Spirit, whom the Father will send in my name, he will teach you all things and bring to your remembrance all that I have said to you." (John 14:26 ESV)

Having a Strong Faith in God

The very moment we trust in Jesus we start living a life of victory. Through faith in Jesus, we find absolute hope and purpose. Learning to trust in Him will change your life forever. Jesus is all that we need. When we commit to Jesus, we can trust in Him to act on our behalf.

You can have faith that God will do marvelous things when you trust in Him in spite of your current circumstances. No matter what situation you may encounter in life, you can trust that all things work together for the good of those who love God. Although we will go through many hardships to enter the kingdom of God, we can have full assurance that we are blessed when we put our trust in God. Without God's grace, we would be lost, but through the death of Jesus on the Cross, all who believe in Him receive eternal life. It is only by the sacrifice Jesus made for us and by His amazing grace and unfailing love that we can come boldly before God's throne.

As believers, we are called to strengthen the body of Christ by encouraging and praying for each other. I know that prayer changes things because I have seen God's mighty hand at work answering so many of my prayers. He has been faithful to me and has carried me through many storms. I am certain it is by God's powerful might that we are guarded from evil. He hears and answers our prayers and is always waiting with open arms for us.

To develop and nurture our intimate relationship with God, we must make a commitment to be still before Him and to wait patiently for Him while praying and studying His Word. When we trust Him, He is faithful, and we can have assurance that everything will work out for the good for those who love Him, those who are called according to His purpose.

"The Lord is good to those whose hope is in him, to the one who seeks him." (Lamentations 3:25 NIV)

Frequent Reasons for Unanswered Prayers

There were so many times in my life when I could not help but question why God was delaying the answer I was praying for, but in every situation, without exception, He always had a good reason for what seemed like a delay. I thank God for all of my unanswered prayers. Now I realize that His will and His timing are perfect and my motives and my desires are not. Keep in mind a no from God can be one of the best answers that He could ever give you.

As Christians, we have the privilege to receive answers to our prayers, but regardless of God's eagerness to answer our prayers, some prayers still go unanswered. There are many reasons why our prayers go unanswered, and some of them may have to do with our lack of knowledge of God's will, lack of fellowship with God, choices, behavior, faith, improper motives, failure to apply spiritual authority, not knowing how to pray, or un-confessed sin.

Unanswered prayers can be a result of a lack of fellowship with the Lord. When we spend time reading the Word of God and in prayer, we can have confidence that we will see answers to our prayers because we are staying in fellowship and allowing God's Word to remain in us.

"If you abide in me, and my words abide in you, ask whatever you wish, and it will be done for you." (John 15:7 ESV)

Unanswered prayers can be a result of not pleasing God. We will receive answers to our prayers, by demonstrating love to others. God commanded that we are to love the Lord with all our heart, mind, and soul and to love our neighbor as ourselves. Because faith works by love, the lack of love, or holding on to bitterness, and un-forgiveness is the root of many unanswered prayers.

"And receive from him anything we ask. We receive it because we obey his commandments and do what pleases him." (1 John 3:22 GW)

Unanswered prayers can be a result of sin. I have no doubt in my mind that sin disrupts the flow of God's blessings and answers to our prayer. Remember all acts of rebellion and disobedience towards God are considered sin, so when we have sin in our life, the Lord will not answer us. The remedy is to confess those sins to God, turn away from them, and ask for forgiveness.

"For the eyes of the Lord are on the righteous and his ears are attentive to their prayer, but the face of the Lord is against those who do evil." (1 Peter 3:12 TNIV)

Unanswered prayers can be a result of asking with wrong motives. God wishes to answer our prayers, but sometimes what we ask for will merely feed our physical, worldly, and selfish pleasures. Our motives and desires can be corrected by making a decision that the Bible is the final authority for our thoughts, motives, decisions, and actions.

"You ask and do not receive, because you ask with wrong motives, so that you may spend it on your pleasures." (James 4:3 NASB)

Unanswered prayers can be a result of not asking in God's will. God's will is revealed through out the Bible. We can be confident that God is faithful to grant us our prayers, petitions, and requests when we ask for things that are in His Will. Make the time to study God's Word so you know what His will is and what His promises are.

"We are confident that God listens to us if we ask for anything that has his approval. We know that he listens to our requests. So we know that we already have what we ask him for." (1 John 5:14-15 GW)

Unanswered prayers can be a result of not knowing how to pray. Prayer is a conversation with God. You talk, and He listens. Then He talks, and you listen. It is a private, intimate time with the Lord. Prayer is a time to present our needs, and desires, and the needs of others before God.

"When you pray, go to your room and close the door. Pray privately to your Father who is with you. Your Father sees what you do in private. He will reward you." (Matthew 6:6 GW)

Unanswered prayers can be a result of a lack of faith. Without faith, it is impossible to please God. Our faith grows as we devote our attention to the Word of God, and diligently seek a personal relationship with Him. To receive from God our faith must become constant, solid, and unshakable. There are those who allow every emotion, situation, or incident to sway their faith. One minute they believe, but the next, they are prepared to give up. They base their faith on their feelings or opinions instead of God's Word. We must have faith when we pray that we have received an answer at that moment, believing in the finished results of our prayers, even though we may not see the answer at that moment. Eventually, we will see the tangible results.

"Now faith is confidence in what we hope for and assurance about what we do not see." (Hebrews 11:1 NIV)

Unanswered prayers can be a result of giving up. Sometimes we give up praying before we receive our answers. We are blessed to have the promise of God's Word, so be patient. Keep believing and praying. God has a perfect time when He will answer our prayers.

"We can't allow ourselves to get tired of living the right way. Certainly, each of us will receive everlasting life at the proper time, if we don't give up." (Galatians 6:9 GW)

Unanswered prayers can be a result of our failure to apply spiritual authority. Our prayers may need to engage in spiritual warfare by using our God-given authority to speak directly to the mountains, obstacles, or problems and command the Devil to move in the name of Jesus. Remember that we do not wrestle against flesh and blood but against principalities, against powers, against the rulers of the darkness of this age, against spiritual hosts of wickedness in the heavenly places.

"I can guarantee this truth: This is what will be done for someone who doesn't doubt but believes what he says will happen: He can say to this mountain, 'Be uprooted and thrown into the sea,' and it will be done for him." (Mark 11:23 GW)

Praise and give thanks and sometimes fast while you are praying to strengthen your faith and your God-given spiritual authority of your prayer. Pray with confidence, expecting to receive answered prayers.

CHAPTER 2

The Importance of Praising God

As children of God, we are instructed to praise God for whom He is and what He has done. We should give Him all our praise and magnify Him through our words, actions, and everyday life. God requires His holy name to be highly esteemed. It is our obligation that we not only agree with God's Word but also obey it by honoring and magnifying Him. We must be willing to display the honor and glory that's due to Him. The Word of God is absolute. Therefore, our reaction to Scripture's truth should be faithful obedience to honor, praise, and magnify Him at all costs, even in the face of opposition and criticism.

Giving glory and praise to God is a wonderful thing. When we give glory and praise to God, we lift Him up. When we praise and magnify Him, we can't help but have humble hearts. It's amazing what a little praise will do for our countenances, our spirits, and the heart of God.

One way to give God praise is verbally. This happens in prayer, a conversation with God, just talking to Him. When we talk of the good things that He does, we magnify Him above our problems. So, the next time you want to give glory and praise to God while you pray, consider telling Him how great He is or thank Him for what He has done for you.

Praise is our greatest weapon of spiritual warfare. God and our enemy cannot be glorified in the same place or at the same time, so when we are praising God, evil must flee. When we give God glory and praise and magnify Him, we draw closer to God, and we make Him bigger than any problem we are experiencing.

Scriptures that Magnify God

"I will bow down toward your holy temple and will praise your name for your unfailing love and your faithfulness, for you have so exalted your solemn decree that it surpasses your fame." (Psalm 138:2 NIV)

"Through Jesus, therefore, let us continually offer to God a sacrifice of praise—the fruit of lips that openly profess his name." (Hebrews 13:15 NIV)

"But you are a chosen people, a royal priesthood, a holy nation, God's special possession, that you may declare the praises of him who called you out of darkness into his wonderful light." (1 Peter 2:9 NIV)

"I will praise God's name in song and glorify him with thanksgiving." (Psalm 69:30 NIV)

"I will give thanks to you, LORD, with all my heart; I will tell of all your wonderful deeds. I will be glad and rejoice in you; I will sing the praises of your name, O Most High." (Psalm 9:1-2 NIV)

"I will extol the LORD at all times; his praise will always be on my lips. I will glory in the LORD; let the afflicted hear and rejoice. Glorify the LORD with me; let us exalt his name together." (Psalm 34:1-3 NIV)

"I will give thanks to the LORD because of his righteousness; I will sing the praises of the name of the LORD Most High." (Psalm 7:17 NIV)

Prayers to Reverence God

Exalting the Character of God

Heavenly Father, I praise You for who You are. I am so grateful that You are personal. You possess all the qualities of personality, intelligence, emotions, self-will, and humor. You are eternal. You are from everlasting to everlasting. You can see the end from the beginning. You are never surprised by anything. You are God Almighty, You created the universe. I worship You as my Creator. You are self existent. You have no beginning or end. In the beginning You were already there.

Father God, You are Spirit, which does not exist in a body that can be seen or touched, so when I worship You, I will worship You in Spirit and in truth. You are the Godhead, the Father, Son, and Holy Spirit. Although, You reveal Yourself in three persons, You are one and cannot be divided. You are unchallengeable. You are the same yesterday, today, and forever.

Gracious Father, You are self-sufficient. You have no needs and there is no way You can improve. You do not need our help with anything, but because of Your grace and love, You allow us to be a part of advancing Your kingdom on earth. You are wisdom. You make no mistakes. You are the Father who truly knows best, that is why it is impossible for us to understand Your decisions and Your ways. You are infinite and You know no boundaries. You are without measure. You are holiness. Your holiness sets You apart from all creation. There is absolutely no sin or evil thought in You.

Father God, You are Sovereignty. You have been and will always be in control of all history. You are absolutely free to do what You know to be best. You are in control of everything that happens. Yet You still give us free will over our choices. You are all-knowing. Everything that happens is under Your control; there is nothing hidden from You. Even when I do not understand I trust in Your perfect plan. Your knowledge will always surpass all understanding.

Father God, You are all powerful, Your Word is so powerful that it can transform every life. I believe there is power in Your Word to make that which is not seen become known. You are everywhere, whether nearby or far away. You fill heaven and earth, no matter where I go or what I do, You are there. You are unchallengeable. You will never change or fade away. You are loving and true at all times. You offer miracles and freedom to Your children.

Heavenly Father, I praise You for all that You are. Your goodness and compassion to me causes me to offer my praises to You. You are righteous and just dealing fairly with all Your children. You are faithful; everything that You have promised will come to pass. You do not lie. It is on Your faithfulness that my hope of eternal life rests. I am convinced that You will honor Your promise that my sins are forgiven and that I will live forever with You.

Father God, You are love. You hold the well-being of others as Your primary concern. I am certain the sacrifice at the cross of Calvary is the ultimate act of love. Your love is not a love of emotion but of action. Your love gives freely to those who choose to follow You. You are mercy. You generously show mercy to all those who have chosen Jesus as their Savior. You are goodness. You are kind, approachable, compassionate, and full of integrity. You bestow blessings on Your followers. You are gracious. You enjoy giving excellent gifts to those who love You, even when we do not deserve it. I am so grateful for Your grace.

In the precious name of Jesus I pray. Amen.

"The LORD is good to all; he has compassion on all he has made." (Psalm 145:9 NIV)

Praise and Glory to Your Mighty Name

Father God, in Your name I put all my trust. I declare that Your name is good. I am convinced those who acknowledge Your name can trust in You because You have never forsaken those who pursue You. I have faith that all who take refuge in You shall be glad and forever sing for joy. I am certain those who love You know how to rejoice.

Father God, I declare that in You alone will I boast all day long. I will give praise and glory to Your mighty name eternally for what You have done for me. Blessed are those who have learned to respect You and walk in the light of Your presence. I rejoice in Your name all day long and triumph in Your righteousness. I will not turn away from You because I depend on You.

Holy Spirit, teach me Your ways so I know how to walk in the truth. Revive me and give me an undivided heart so I may keep God's law as long as I live.

Father God, with uplifted hands, I proclaim glory to Your faithful name. I hope the hearts of those who seek You rejoice as my heart rejoices. I trust You early in the morning as I think about how faithful and praiseworthy You are. I express thankfulness in the evening as I lay my burdens at Your feet. With my lips, I declare my gratefulness, and because of Your righteousness, I sing praise to Your name.

Father God, all the earth fears Your name and bows down; it sings praise to Your majestic name. I pray You will spread Your protection over Your people and gather us from the nations. Call out to this lost and rebellious generation. Cover their faces with shame and open their eyes to see the truth that will set them free. I pray that this nation will repent, and all the nations will come and worship before You and proclaim Your salvation day after day. I praise You for who You are. I will continually sing praises to Your name because You are good, gracious, and lovely.

In the precious name of Jesus I pray. Amen.

"Praise the Lord, for the Lord is good; sing praise to his name, for that is pleasant." (Psalm 135:3 NIV)

Modelling the Prayer that Jesus Taught

Heavenly Father, You are the only true living God. You are the Father who reigns in heaven. You are above all, the Kings of kings and the

Lord of lords. I proclaim Your name is great and greatly to be praised. I honor, worship, and praise Your mighty name.

Father God, I declare Your divine reign over my life. I long for Your kingdom to come and Christ to return and establish a new heaven and earth. I proclaim You rule over the whole universe and Your sovereignty is eternal.

Father God, I desire for Your prefect, all-knowing will to be done in my life. I consent to Your perfect purpose to be fulfilled in and through me for all eternity. I am grateful that Your will, shall be done on earth as it is in heaven. I am thankful You are my provider and You supply all of my daily needs. I declare You meet all my needs according to Your glorious riches in Christ Jesus.

Father God, thank You for forgiving me of all of my sins and cleansing me of my mistakes. I declare I have forgiven those who have hurt or mistreated me. I will continue to forgive others who sin against me. I pray You will give me the strength to move on from my past failures and pains. I am confident if I forgive other people when they sin against me, I will also be forgiven.

Father God. I pray You will keep me far from all sin and give me the courage to turn away from temptation. I understand that Satan will tempt me with everything imaginable. I pray You will help me to recognize and overcome the temptation by following Your ways. I pray You will keep me safe in Your loving arms, release angels to encamp around me, and build a hedge of protection to surround me.

Father God, I acknowledge that You are a powerful living King who is majestic and will reign for eternity. I declare that all dominion belongs to You. You have authority over all, and no one can defeat You. You are magnificent, and all the praise, honour and glory belong to You. Forever and ever, You are and will always be Lord of my life.

In the precious name of Jesus I pray. Amen.

"This, then, is how you should pray: Our Father in heaven, hallowed be your name, your kingdom come, your will be done, on earth as it is in heaven. Give us today our daily bread. And forgive us our debts, as we also have forgiven our debtors." (Matthew 6:9-12 NIV)

Offering a Sacrifice of Praise

Lord Jesus, I proclaim You are my Lord, Master and Savior. My Prince of Peace and Redeemer, all power and glory belongs to You. I reverently give You all my praise and admiration. I declare I will continually offer to You a sacrifice of praise. With the fruit of my lips, I will openly profess Your name.

Father God, I believe You are Spirit and I worship You in spirit and in truth. I offer my body as a living sacrifice. I trust this is holy and pleasing to You and is true and proper worship. As I worship, my heart is filled with joy, gladness, and thanksgiving.

Heavenly Father, I worship You with reverence and awe. I am grateful that You have blessed me in Your heavenly kingdom with every spiritual blessing in Christ Jesus. I declare I am an heir of Your kingdom that cannot be shaken and I offer my sacrifice of praise.

Father God, I am certain when You spoke, You created the universe. By Your great power and outstretched arms, nothing is too hard for You. I am convinced whatever is impossible with man is possible with You. No matter how great a problem I am facing. I have faith there is no obstacles that is insoluble to You. I have seen You work Your great power on my behalf. For that reason, I offer You praise and I am able to trust You even more.

In the precious name of Jesus I pray. Amen.

"Through Jesus, therefore, let us continually offer to God a sacrifice of praise, the fruit of lips that openly profess his name." (Hebrews 13:15 NIV)

CHAPTER 3

Praying for Children

As mature Christians, we need to make a commitment to invest in the next generation. The legacy we should leave behind is wholehearted devotion and passion for Christ, taking the time to share with children the beliefs and values that have been fundamental to our spiritual growth. We need to help them realize the awesome thing God did when He created them and acknowledge the talents God has given them.

Remember that we build character in our children by building up our children. Focus on their strong points, not their weaknesses. By our words, we can speak blessings or curses over them. Make the choice to pray blessings over children. God's Word tells us, "This day I call the heavens, and the earth as witnesses against you, that I have set before you life and death, blessings, and curses. Now choose life, so that you and your children may live." (Deuteronomy 30:19 NLT)

We should show them that our love for them is unconditional as God loves us. We should pray for them daily, covering our children in prayer before they go out into the world. Pray that they are able to make the right decisions and stay away from all that is evil.

Remember that every soul is cherished by our loving Father and children's souls are precious. The loss of their souls would be dreadful. The thought that our prayers may be instrumental to their eternity should stir us up to offer continuous prayer on their behalf.

Even if you do not have children of your own, there are always children you could pray for. We may be the only Jesus that child sees. Seeing

God's love in the face of another person can make a huge difference to a child. God notices every act of kindness and appreciates it. We need to be sure that we are sharing God's love by showing it.

Scripture for Children

"Start children off on the way they should go, and even when they are old they will not turn from it." (Proverbs 22:6 NIV)

"Children, obey your parents in the Lord, for this is right. 'Honor your father and mother,' which is the first commandment with a promise 'so that it may go well with you and that you may enjoy long life on the earth." (Ephesians 6:1-3 NIV)

"Children, obey your parents in everything, for this pleases the Lord." (Colossians 3:20 NIV)

"Discipline your children, and they will give you peace; they will bring you the delights you desire." (Proverbs 29:17 NIV)

"Fathers, do not exasperate your children; instead, bring them up in the training and instruction of the Lord." (Ephesians 6:4 NIV)

"All your children shall be taught by the Lord, and great shall be the peace of your children." (Isaiah 54:13 ESV)

"If you obey all the decrees and commands I am giving you today, all will be well with you and your children. I am giving you these instructions so you will enjoy a long life in the land the Lord your God is giving you for all time." (Deuteronomy 4:40 NLT)

Prayers for Children

Developing God-Given Gifts and Talents

Father God, I thank You for the gifts and talents that You have placed in my children. I pray that they will use them for Your glory and develop them in Your timing. I have faith that the gifts and callings You have placed on them are irrevocable. I pray that my children will recognize and implement the gifts that You have placed on their lives. I pray their gifts and talents never glorify anyone or anything besides You. I pray that my children will be strong in their beliefs and their commitments toward You.

Father God, I am so grateful that You give the gift of the Holy Spirit to those who ask You. I pray that You will baptize my children with the gifts of the Holy Spirit. I have faith that the gifts of the Holy Spirit will be distributed according to Your will. I pray You will encourage my children to use their gifts according to the grace that You have given them. I pray that no feeling of fear, inadequacy, uncertainty will keep them from using their talents and gifts.

Father God, help my children to excel in the plans that You have for them. Keep them on the path of righteousness and bless the works of their hands. I pray that they will help and encourage people with their talents. I pray that they will be successful in school and at work and that they will experience prosperous lives. I am confident that a man's gift makes room for him and brings him before great men. I pray my children will find favor, first of all with You and then with people.

Holy Spirit, I pray You will direct and encourage my children to get the spiritual and academic education that they need to develop the talents God has placed in them. Inspire them to pursue a deep thirst for knowledge. Provide opportunities for them to serve in the church and their community.

In the precious name of Jesus I pray. Amen.

"If you then, though you are evil, know how to give good gifts to your children, how much more will your Father in heaven give the Holy Spirit to those who ask him." (Luke 11:13 NIV)

Obtaining Knowledge, Wisdom, and Understanding

Father God, I believe that You give wisdom and from Your mouth comes knowledge and understanding. I pray You will help my children to see that with wisdom a house is built, and with understanding it is established, and with knowledge its rooms are filled with every kind of treasures. I pray that You will open their eyes and hearts to receive knowledge, wisdom, and understanding of Your Word and Your will.

Holy Spirit, help my children to discern between God's will and their own. Encourage them to read the Bible and assist them in developing knowledge of the Word. I pray they will desire God's Word as a newborn baby needs milk. I declare that the truth shall set them free and God's Word gives my children wisdom for their decisions.

Father God, I pray that my children will see through Your eyes, hear with Your ears, comprehend with the mind of Jesus, and speak Your Word with boldness. I pray their mouths will speak words of wisdom. I pray that the Holy Spirit will guide my children and Jesus will be the light of their lives. I am certain when they acknowledge You in all their ways, You shall direct their paths. Thank You for watching over them, for showing them where to go. I pray they will have the wisdom to only walk through doors that You have opened for them.

Father God, I am convinced that You want everyone to be saved and to come to know the knowledge of Your truth. I pray that my children will grow in their salvation and in the knowledge of Jesus Christ. I believe when they reflect on Your Word, You will help them understand all things.

Abba Father, I pray my children will be fruitful in every good work, increasing in the knowledge of You. I declare when my children lack wisdom, they can ask, and You will give it to them generously. I have faith they will grow in knowledge, wisdom, and understanding of Your Word and Your ways for Your kingdom's cause.

In the precious name of Jesus I pray. Amen.

"For the LORD gives wisdom; from his mouth come knowledge and understanding." (Proverbs 2:6 NIV)

Raising Daughters after God's Own Heart

Father God, I declare that my daughters are Your daughters and they are heirs with Christ Jesus. They are virtuous women and they hold on to moral excellence. I pray that they will fear You and desire to have Your favor on their lives more than that of man. I pray they will renew their minds in Your Word daily. I pray my daughters keep Your commands and abide in Your love so their surroundings are filled with Your love.

Holy Spirit, encourage my daughters to take on the mind of Christ. I pray they will realize that apart from Jesus, they can do nothing. I pray they will desire the sincere milk of the Word so that they grow in the things of God. I pray they will want God's perfect will for their lives and they walk in a manner that is worthy of it.

Heavenly Father, I proclaim their minds are gifted, their eyesight is bright, their health is outstanding, and their intellectual capacity is abundant. I declare they take exceptional consideration of their bodies because they acknowledge that their bodies are a temple of the Holy Spirit. I declare they are godly woman and they have self-respect, so they dress appropriately.

Father God, I pray my daughters will live the kind of lives that prove they belong to Jesus, and they will want to please Him in every way as they grow, producing every kind of good work as they come to know Him more intimately. I declare they manage their school, chores, and work with godly wisdom. I am certain that they are empowered with wisdom to resolve challenges because You give them ideas, concepts, and inventions, and they have discernment, and understanding in all things.

Father God, I declare my daughters have the power to obtain wealth and they have more than enough. They handle money wisely because they first seek Your wisdom. They do not waste precious time sitting around. They take care of all that needs taking care of in a timely and efficient manner.

Father God, I have faith because they are Your daughters, they have the right to come confidently before Your throne and obtain answers to their prayers. I declare they are prayer warriors and they believe and speak Your Word over everything. I have confidence every word You speak, they can trust in and rely on. Thank You for all the blessings You give my daughters.

In the precious name of Jesus I pray. Amen.

"Do you not know that your bodies are temples of the Holy Spirit, who is in you, whom you have received from God? You are not your own." (1 Corinthians 6:19 NIV)

Raising Sons to Become Godly Men

Father God, I proclaim that my sons are Your sons and they will enjoy the promise of Your blessings because they belong to Jesus. I pray they will make the time to renew their minds in Your Word each day and they will keep Your commands and remain in Your love. I pray they will take on the mind of Christ, realizing that apart from Jesus, they can do nothing.

Father God, I am confident they have the right to come boldly before Your throne of grace and receive answers to their prayers. I declare my sons are victorious prayer warriors and they trust and speak Your Word over all their circumstances. I am grateful they can trust in and rely on Your Word.

Father God, I pray that they will fear You and desire to have Your favor on their lives more than that of man. I pray my sons will desire Your perfect will for their lives and they will walk in a way that is worthy of it. I am confident my sons are empowered with wisdom to resolve problems because You give them ideas, concepts, and inventions. I pray they will use discernment and understanding in all areas of their lives.

Father God, I pray the way my sons behave will always delight You and their achievement will generate victory and they will mature as they learn to know You more. I declare they handle their education, responsibilities, and work with godly insight. I declare they have the power to achieve wealth. They have more than enough and they handle money wisely because they first seek Your wisdom. I pray they will not squander precious time on wasteful habits or ungodly pastimes. I declare they take care of all their everyday jobs in a timely and professional manner.

Heavenly Father, I proclaim my sons take excellent care of their bodies because they recognize their bodies are a temple of the Holy Spirit for that reason, the Holy Spirit's light shines in them. I declare their minds are clever and intellectual, their eyesight is clear, their health is excellent, their comprehension is strong, and they are victorious men, and they hold honest qualities, and self-respect.

In the precious name of Jesus I pray. Amen.

"Then the way you live will always honor and please the Lord, and your lives will produce every kind of good fruit. All the while, you will grow as you learn to know God better and better." (Colossians 1:10 NIV)

Living for Your Kingdom

Father God, I come boldly before Your throne of grace. I pray that You will make use of my children for Your kingdom's cause. I pray like little children they will come to You and that no one will be able to hinder them. I am confident that the kingdom of heaven belongs to such as these. I am grateful when they become followers of Jesus they become part of Your heavenly kingdom.

Father God, I pray that You will give my children divine encounters and favor from everyone that they meet. Assign them ministry positions that You have planned for them before the beginning of time. I pray that You will open doors of opportunity that no man can shut and that You will close the doors that are not of Your will. Give my children dreams, visions, and wisdom. Encourage them to look ahead and not behind.

Heavenly Father, I pray that every word that comes out of their mouths is pleasing to You. I pray their words, actions, and deeds give You glory. I declare that health, joy, wisdom, and prosperity belong to them. I declare that my children are wonderfully blessed and highly favored by You first and then by man. I pray that they will live for Your kingdom's cause and always seek Your approval in all that they do.

Father God, thank You for Your unconditional love and the abundant blessings You have showered upon my children. I declare that You are the light for their path and You know the plans that You have for them, plans to give them hope and a excellent future. I am so grateful that Your ways are not their ways and Your thoughts are not their thoughts. I am certain that Your ways are more than they could ever have hoped for or imagined.

In the precious name of Jesus I pray. Amen.

"Jesus said, 'Let the little children come to me, and do not hinder them, for the kingdom of heaven belongs to such as these." (Matthew 19:14 NIV)

Heartfelt Repentance

Father God, I pray that You will give my children hearts that are quick to confess their mistakes. I pray they will sincerely regret their past sins and will earnest desire to walk in a new path of righteousness. I have confidence You will cleanse and forgive them. I pray that I will be an example to them, living a life that reflects true repentance.

Holy Spirit, help my children to see that those who conceal their sins do not prosper but those who confess and renounce them find mercy. Help my children to refrain from making the same mistakes over and over again. Give them the strength to turn from any sinful habits. I pray You will bring to their attention any sins that they are holding on to. I pray You will motivate them to confess their sins so that they can be forgiven.

Father God, cleanse my children from their sins and iniquities. I pray they will have genuine heartfelt repentance. Create new hearts in them, and fill them with a spirit of hope, love, joy, peace, and self-control. I pray that they will know beyond any doubt that You are true and just to forgive when they confess and turn from those sins. I pray that You saturate them with a spirit of honesty. I pray that the words they speak and the actions they take are pleasing in Your sight.

Gracious Heavenly Father, I have confidence that blessed are those whose transgressions are forgiven, whose sins are covered. I pray my children will not live in condemnation. I pray they will truly comprehend that the grace of the Lord Jesus Christ, the fellowship of the Holy Spirit, and Your unconditional love are always with them, and that Your grace is sufficient.

In the precious name of Jesus I pray. Amen.

"Whoever conceals their sins does not prosper, but the one who confesses and renounces them finds mercy." (Proverbs 28:13 NIV)

Entering the Kingdom of Heaven

Heavenly Father, I present my request before You. I lay my children at Your feet. I pray that my children will grow in the grace and the knowledge of my Lord and Savior, Jesus Christ. I am confident we cannot be saved until You call us. I pray You will invite my children to join You. I am certain that Jesus came to call all sinners to repentance. Thank You for loving the world so much that You gave Your one and only son so that whosoever believes in Jesus shall not perish but will have everlasting life. I pray Your light will shine into their darkness.

Holy Spirit, I have faith that a man's heart plans his way, but God directs his steps. I pray You will guide my children in the right way and lead them down a smooth path. Help them to stand firm and not be burdened down by the yoke of slavery. Rather, let them clothe themselves with the Lord Jesus. Encourage them to not merely listen to the Word but strengthen them to do what the Word teaches. I pray that You give them revelation so that they can cast off restraints. I pray they will not be misled by bad company that will corrupt their spirits.

Father God, I declare that Christ has set us free and my children shall rejoice in that freedom. I pray they will not think about how to gratify the desires of their sinful nature but they will humble themselves under Your mighty hand so that they may be exalted by You in due time. I pray that my children will fix their eyes on Jesus, the author and finisher of their faith, so they will not grow weary and lose heart. I pray they will open their eyes to see Your glory.

Heavenly Father, unless we change and become like little children, we will never enter the kingdom of heaven. Thank You for the promise that all who trust Jesus as their Lord and Savior have the right to become Your children. I pray that my children will receive Jesus while they are young and that they will not depart from Him all the days of their lives. I ask that You sanctify my children by Your truth.

Father God, help my children to see that the power of life and death is in their tongues and by their words they will be declared innocent or by their words they will be declared guilty. I pray my children will confess that they have been crucified in Christ and they no longer live but Jesus lives in them. I declare they shall rejoice because their names are written in heaven. I pray they will choose to love You with their whole hearts, minds, souls, and with all their strength. Thank You for the good work You have started in them. I have faith You will see it through to completion.

In the precious name of Jesus I pray. Amen.

"And he said: 'Truly I tell you, unless you change and become like little children, you will never enter the kingdom of heaven." (Matthew 18:3 NIV)

Establishing an Eternal Future

Gracious Heavenly Father, it brings joy to my soul to know that You are faithful with Your promises. I am confident in the truth of Your Word. I believe that Your desire is for all to come to know Jesus as their Lord and Savior. I pray You will reveal to my children that Jesus is the only way to receive eternal life and they must trust in the Lord Jesus to be saved. I have faith that because I believe in the Lord Jesus, my entire household will be saved.

Father God, I declare my children will come to know the knowledge of Your saving grace while they are young. I bring my children before You today and ask that You give them revelation to understand who You really are. Open the eyes of their hearts and let Your light shine in. I pray that my children will fully comprehend Your forgiveness and any guilt or failure they may feel will leave their minds and hearts. I break the spirit of death off of them and deposit in them the desire to have eternal life.

Father God, I pray that my children will have the faith to confess with their mouths that Jesus is their Lord and believe in their hearts that You raised Jesus from the dead. I am certain You make everything beautiful in its time and that You have put eternity in their hearts. Now it is up to them to receive it. I pray You will pour out Your Spirit upon them. Give them spiritual understanding so they will receive the baptism of the Holy Spirit.

Holy Spirit, encourage my children to fix their eyes not on what is seen but on what is unseen. Reveal to them that what is seen is temporary but what is unseen is eternal. Guide their paths and accompany them in the right direction. Grant them wisdom and discernment and reveal the truth to them. I pray they will receive eternity into their hearts today and that they will never slide away from it. I pray they will follow Jesus forever and will walk in a way that is pleasing to God.

In the precious name of Jesus I pray. Amen.

"He has made everything beautiful in its time. He has also set eternity in the human heart; yet no one can fathom what God has done from beginning to end." (Ecclesiastes 3:11 NIV)

Building a Strong Faith

Heavenly Father, I have confidence that You have given my children the faith that they need. I pray that You will reveal to them that faith in You assures them of the things they expect and convince them of the things they cannot see. I am certain You have given us all a measure of faith and all we need is faith the size of a mustard seed and we can move mountains.

Holy Spirit, help my children to build a strong faith in God. Encourage them to deepen their faith by tapping into the truth of God's Word so their faith will grow. I pray that they will attend church so they will hear the good news about Christ and learn of His faithfulness.

Father God, I believe that those who serve You will gain an excellent standing and great assurance in their faith through Christ Jesus. I pray my children will draw near to You with a sincere heart. Understanding the full assurance that faith brings, having their hearts spiritually sprinkled to cleanse them from guilty consciences and having their bodies washed with pure water.

Father God, I am confident if they wait patiently, You will turn to them and hear their prayers. I am sure that when my children ask for anything that is according to Your will, all things whatsoever they ask for in prayer while they believe they shall receive. I have confidence their, spiritual weapons are mighty, and the authority of Jesus is far greater than the power of darkness so the Enemy must yield. I pray that my children will take hold of the spiritual authority that You have given them and all bondage will be destroyed because their faith has set them free.

Father God, I exercise the authority You have granted me to rebuke the Devourer so that he will not destroy my children. I take that authority. I annihilate Satan's strongholds from my children lives. I extinguish all curses that have been spoken against them from affecting their minds, health, happiness, finances, and their walk with You.

In the precious name of Jesus I pray. Amen.

"Now faith is confidence in what we hope for and assurance about what we do not see." (Hebrews 11:1 NIV)

Rescued, Restored, and Set Free

Gracious Heavenly Father, I pray that You will give my children the peace that they need, Your peace that surpasses all understanding. I cast down and demolish every argument and every pretension that sets itself against the knowledge of You. I proclaim that my children are Your workmanship created in Christ Jesus to do the good works that You prepared for them in advance.

Father God, I believe in Your Word and I trust in Your promises. I believe that my children will be rescued and set free because Your Word teaches me if I believe in the Lord, Jesus Christ, my whole family will be saved. I am certain that You will send a messenger by which my whole family will be saved. Thank You for the protection that You have set around them. I have comfort in knowing that You contend with those who contend with me and that my children shall be saved.

Holy Spirit, I pray You will encourage my children to look ahead and not behind and You will take captive their every thought to make them obedient to Christ. Reveal to them that salvation is God's plan to provide us an escape from the consequences of sin and is the only way for them to be truly saved, healed, delivered, pardoned, rescued, protected, preserved, made whole, cured, set free, and restored.

Father God, I am so grateful that I can ask and it will be given to me, and when I seek I will find, and when I knock the door will be opened to me. I pray that You will use my children mightily for Your kingdom. Give them divine encounters and ministry positions that You have predestined for them before the foundation of this world.

Father God, I pray that my children will have favor first with You and then with men. I pray that You will open doors of opportunity for them that no man can shut. I pray that every word that comes out of their mouths is acceptable to You and their words, actions, and deeds will give You glory. I declare that health, happiness, and prosperity are theirs. I pray for victory, peace, wholeness, and healing for my children. I declare that they belong to Jesus. They are restored, set free, born again, water baptized, and filled with the Holy Spirit.

In the precious name of Jesus I pray. Amen.

"But this is what the Lord says: 'Yes, captives will be taken from warriors, and plunder retrieved from the fierce; I will contend with those who contend with you, and your children I will save." (Isaiah 49:25 NIV)

The Perfect Wife for My Son

Father God, I pray that my son will see that marriage should be viewed as a godly tradition. I pray that You will prepare my son for his wife and prepare her for him. Prevent my son from entering into marriage carelessly, without serious reflection on the consequences of his choice. Reveal to him when a man enters into a marriage, he makes a vow, a vow that he is required to keep. I declare when my son finds a wife he will find a good thing and obtain favor from You. I am confident that an excellent wife is the crown to her husband, and it is You who gives a man a virtuous and prudent wife.

Holy Spirit, encourage my son to make his choice cautiously and on the basis of her godly character. Help him to see that a man who marries a devout wife has a wife who will bring honor to him, and she is truly a helper to him. Reveal to my son that when he loves and honors his wife as he should, it creates the best environment for his wife to fulfill her role as a faithful helper. I pray that his wife will do him good and not evil all the days of their lives.

Father God, I am certain that the ideal wife is set apart as a woman of wisdom, one who opens her mouth with wisdom and the teaching of kindness are on her tongue. I pray You will prepare for him a wife that will be faithful to him. Let him have comfort in knowing that his heart can trust in her. I pray that she will have a gracious spirit, and open her heart, and her home with love, and kindness.

Father God, encourage him to be a wise husband full of kindness, honesty, generosity, and forgiveness. I pray that my son will be a peacemaker, he will exercise self-control, and have a positive outlook on life, and he will speak with a gentle tongue. I pray that he will fear You and that he is obedient to Your Word. I pray my son will possess a humble spirit, and will be willing to listen to counsel, and admit when he is wrong.

Heavenly Father, I pray my son will be a godly leader of his home, that he will not be a jealous man, and that he will always be faithful, and reliable to his wife and family. I pray that they will live a life that is pleasing before You, and they will raise their children to love, and serve You. I declare that my son is a hardworking man with a successful career. I pray that he will understand that You are the one who gives him the ability to produce wealth. I pray they will recognize the importance of tithing, and giving, and that they will have a concern for others, especially the poor and the oppressed.

In the precious name of Jesus I pray. Amen.

"She speaks with wisdom, and faithful instruction is on her tongue." (Proverbs 31:26 NIV)

The Ideal Husband for My Daughters

Father God, I pray that my daughters will understand that marriage must be viewed as a divine institution. I pray they will enter into marriage with a serious reflection of the consequences of their decisions. Reveal to them when they join into marriage, they make a promise that they are obligated to keep.

Heavenly Father, I believe their selection of a husband can be either a delight or a disaster. I pray that they will seek after a husband that has a personal relationship with You. I pray they will make their choice carefully and on the basis of his relationship with You. I pray they will be attracted to men of integrity, men who exercise self-control, who has discipline over their temper, who speaks with a gentle tongue, who are peacemakers, and who are willing to forgive.

Father God, I pray my daughters will marry compassionate, honest, and generous, men who have a positive outlook on life. I pray their husbands will be wise with a humble spirit, men who are willing to listen to counsel and admit when they are wrong. I pray that their husbands will not be jealous men and that they will always remain faithful and reliable to their family. I pray that they will be a devout leader of their home and that they will serve You faithfully.

Heavenly Father, I pray their husbands will be diligent men with flourishing professions. I pray they will understand that You are the one who gives them the ability to produce wealth. I pray they will see the significance of tithing and offerings and they will have a heart for others, particularly the unfortunate and the broken. I pray that they will live a life that is pleasing before You and they will raise their children to adore You.

Holy Spirit, encourage my daughters to build their homes by building up their husbands and children. I pray they will bring honor to their husbands by respecting them and truly becomes a helper to them. I pray when they open their mouths, wisdom, and kindness is on their tongues.

In the precious name of Jesus I pray. Amen.

"Husbands, love your wives, just as Christ loved the church and gave himself up for her." (Ephesians 5:25 NIV)

Attracting Godly Friends and Role Models

Father God, I pray that You will bring godly friends and role models into my children's lives. Help them to use wisdom when they are choosing friends. Let their friends be of Your likeness. Help them to see that a righteous man is cautious in friendship but the way of the wicked leads them astray.

Holy Spirit, I have confidence that he who walks with the wise shall be wise but a friend of fools shall become like them. I pray You will draw my children to people of godly influence. Strengthen them to be spirit-inspired toward people. I pray that they will only be persuaded by things of heaven, not things of this world. Help them to meet and make friends that love and resemble Jesus.

Holy Spirit, I pray that they will understand that true love comes from God and when they love others they demonstrate that they have been born of God. Encourage my children to love others with the love that comes from God. I pray they will share the love of Jesus with everyone they meet. I pray any unsaved friends my children spend time with will come to receive Jesus as their Lord and Savior.

Father God, I pray You will assist my children in finding wisdom with eternal companions. I pray they will attract born-again friends and acquaintances and You will bring trustworthy friends into their lives. Deliver them from anyone who has a sinful character and strengthen them to not grieve over those lost friendships. I pray that anyone who is not walking in Your footsteps will be removed from their path. I pray they will not make friends with hot-tempered people or become associated with anyone who is easily angered.

Father God, I pray You will eliminate from my children any un-forgiveness, bad memories, low self-esteem, or loneliness that might cause them to seek after less than God-glorified friendships. I pray that each one of their friendships will give You glory. I pray they will be able to say that their friends are truly a gift from You. I pray that they will understand that unreliable friends can destroy one another but a loving friend will stay closer than family. Reveal to them that Jesus is the best friend they will ever have because He is the only faithful friend that will stick closer than a brother.

In the precious name of Jesus I pray. Amen.

"A righteous man is cautious in friendship, but the way of the wicked leads them astray." (Proverbs 12:26 NIV)

Establishing Good Family Relationships

Father God, I pray for healing and restoration over my children's family relationships. Please open a door to their hearts. Give them the courage and motivation to love unconditionally. Show them that even though their family doesn't look like the ideal picture, You can take a less-than-ideal situation and change a broken legacy. Reveal to my children that You rescued them so that the people they love could have Jesus within their reach. I pray that my children will help their family see and choose heaven.

Father God, I pray that You will transform my children in the creation that You have fashioned them to be, saturating them with the love of Jesus and mold them in to His image. Remove from my children any unresolved feelings and preserve them with Your peace. Flood my children's hearts with love and compassion toward others. Give them the desire to get to know their family better. Show them that those who bring trouble on their families will receive nothing but grief.

Heavenly Father, I pray that my children will be accepted for who they are with all their imperfections. Help their loved ones to see that they are Your work in progress. I pray they will develop a close, happy, peaceful, and truthful relationship with family members. Encourage them to respect, appreciate, and admire their family. I pray my children's relationships today, tomorrow, and forever will remain pleasing in Your sight.

Holy Spirit, teach my children how to forgive and reveal to them true forgiveness. I pray they will take the time to resolve misunderstanding.

I pray they will be the first to say that they are sorry and the first to say, "I forgive." Help them to forget the matter and move forward.

Father God, I pray my children will understand that You want them to live in harmony with everyone, to be sympathetic, and loving towards others, having a heart of compassion, and a humble spirit. I pray that You will remove the wedges that Satan has tried to place between family members. I pray You will bring healing and restoration to those relationships. Give my children the desire for reconciliation and take away their prideful self-centered hearts.

In the precious name of Jesus I pray. Amen.

"He who brings trouble on his family will inherit only wind, and the fool will be servant to the wise." (Proverbs 11:29 NIV)

He Who Began a Good Work in You

Gracious Heavenly Father, the confidence that I have in You is that if I ask anything that is according to Your will, You will hear me and answer my prayers. I pray You will reveal to my children Your unfailing love, unshakable faithfulness, steadfast kindness, and eternal grace. I pray that when You stand at the door of their hearts and knock, they will hear You and have the faith and courage to open their hearts so that Your glorious light can shine in.

Father God, I believe that it is Your will for everyone to be saved and that we cannot be saved until You call our names. I pray You will call my children's names quickly. Deal with their hearts and fill them with Your presence. Please do not wait another minute. Shine Your light into their darkness. I pray that my children will trust Jesus as their Savior today and that they will never slide away from Him.

Father God, thank You for the good work You have already begun in them. I am confident You will see it through to its completion and You will never leave their sides. I pray You will multiply them in all area of their lives. I have faith my children will see victory quickly when their hearts choose to serve Christ. I pray they will put You first in all that they do and they will always be eager to do what is right in Your eyes.

In the precious name of Jesus I pray. Amen.

"I'm convinced that God, who began this good work in you, will carry it through to completion on the day of Christ Jesus." (Philippians 1:6 GW)

Wearing the Armor of God

Gracious Heavenly Father, I declare that even though we live in this world, we do not wage war as the world does. The weapons we fight with are not weapons of this world but have divine power to demolish strongholds. I am confident that we have victory over every line of attack that sets itself up against the knowledge of You. We have authority to take captive every thought to make it obedient to Christ.

Holy Spirit, I pray my children will put on the full armor of God. I pray they will be strong in the Lord and in His mighty power so that they can take their stand against the Devil's schemes. I declare that their struggle is not against flesh and blood but against the rulers of darkness, against wicked authorities, against the powers of this dark world, and against the spiritual forces of evil in the heavenly realms.

Father God, I pray my children will put on their full armor so that when the day of evil comes, they will be able to stand their ground. I pray they will stand firm with the belt of truth buckled around their waists, the breastplate of righteousness in place, their feet fitted with the readiness that comes from the gospel of peace. I pray that they will take up the shield of faith, with which they can extinguish all the flaming arrows of the Devil.

Father God, thank You for equipping my children with everything that they need to be spiritually mature. I have confidence that You will bring about deliverance for them. I pray that You will lift them up. Hold them close to You, keeping them under the shadow of Your wings. I pray You will send warring angels out before my children and build a hedge to protect around them.

In the precious name of Jesus I pray. Amen.

The Armor of God: (Ephesians 6:10-16 NIV)

The Spiritual Weapons of Warfare

Father God, thank You for the spiritual weapons You have equipped Your children with. I declare the weapons we fight with are not the weapons of the world. On the contrary, they have divine power to demolish strongholds. I exercise the authority You have granted me over the powers of darkness so that I can cast out demons.

Lord Jesus, in Your name, I command that all spirits that are not the Holy Spirit to depart from my children. I speak to the spirit of fatigue, laziness, and inactivity. I demand them to release my children. I speak to the spirit of complaining, gossip, criticism, untruthfulness, condemnation, deception. I order them to let go of my children. I speak to the spirit of worry, fear, weakness, low self-esteem, doubt, pride, discouragement, distraction. I command them to free my children.

Lord Jesus, in Your name, I speak to the spirit of disrespect, disobedience, stubbornness, strife, discord, rage, hatred, anger, rebellion, wrath, corruption, division. I order them to unleash my children. I speak to the spirit of premarital sex, lust, vanity, selfishness, jealousy. I demand them to set free my children. I speak to the spirit of witchcraft, wickedness, demons, idolatry, distress, occult, strongholds, murder, death, sickness, and any and all ungodly spirits not mentioned by name. I demand they leave my children, never to return again.

Heavenly Father, I speak blessing over my children. I cover them with mercy, grace, love, peace, joy, energy, truth, contentment, kindness, life, unity, humility, honor, thankfulness, wealth, guidance, helpfulness, freedom, integrity, honesty, obedience, eternity, strength, self-esteem, hope, encouragement, health, restoration, angels, and the Holy Spirit. I proclaim that the blood of Jesus covers my children's spirits, souls, and bodies. I release a legion of angels to surround my children wherever they may go. I pray that a hedge of protection will guard and cover them all the days of their lives. I have confidence You are their hiding place, shelter, refuge, fortress, and their ever-present help in times of trouble.

In the precious name of Jesus I pray. Amen.

"The weapons we fight with are not the weapons of the world. On the contrary, they have divine power to demolish strongholds." (2 Corinthians 10:4 NIV)

Covered under God's Hand

Father God, I lift up my children to You. I pray that You will always have a hedge of protection around them. Release their angles to keep them safe for all eternity. Protect their minds, hearts, bodies, and emotions from all harm and evil. I pray for protection from all accidents, evil influences, diseases, sicknesses, injuries, and any physical or emotional abuse. I pray that they will come to understand that they can always find shelter in Your loving arms.

Father God, I pray You will grieve their spirit when evil is near, hide them from any evil influences that might come against them. Keep them aware of all hidden dangers. I declare that no weapon formed against my children shall prosper. I pray You will spread Your hand of protection over them, keeping them safe in all that they do and wherever they go.

Father God, I pray that Christian music, godly entertainment, divine friends, and Your Word will be pleasing to my children's ears, eyes, minds, and spirits. I ask You to remove all the bad influences that they have in their lives right now. I pray that evil of any type, such as music, television, games, Internet, movies, magazines, books, videos, friends, or anything else they may hear, see, or be acquainted with that is not of Your will turns their stomachs.

Father God, I declare my children are the head and not the tail. They are spirit-filled leaders. Your hand protects and guides them in the direction they should go. I have faith that they shall lie down in peace and sleep in stillness because You alone cause them to dwell in safety. I am confident my children are covered and protected under Your mighty hand. I pray they will feel and depend on that safety.

In the precious name of Jesus I pray. Amen.

"But let all who take refuge in you be glad; let them ever sing for joy. Spread your protection over them that those who love your name may rejoice in you." (Psalm 5:11 NIV)

Releasing Ungodly Bondages

Lord Jesus, thank You for the keys to the kingdom of heaven and for the spiritual authority You have given me. I embrace the guarantee that whatever I imprison, God will imprison and whatever I set free, God will set free. I am so grateful that You have anointed Your followers to share the good news to the poor, to comfort the brokenhearted, to proclaim that captives will be released and prisoners will be freed.

Father God, I take my God-given authority. I bind my children's will to Your will. I declare that Your kingdom will come and Your will, shall be done in my children's lives. I join their feelings and emotions to the leading of the Holy Spirit. Help them to realize that their feelings are rarely very trustworthy. Reveal to them You alone know what is in store for them. I pray my children will put all their faith in You instead of trusting their feelings.

Father God, I bind my children's hands to the work that You have ordained for them. I pray they will be happy in their work because it is a gift from You. I bind their feet to the path You have placed before them so that they are in the right place at the right time. I pray in all their ways they will acknowledge You. I have faith You will make their paths straight.

Father God, I bind my children's bodies to the plans and purpose that You placed within them. I am certain they are made in Your Image and their bodies are temples for the Holy Spirit. I bind their lives to the truth that is in Your Word. I pray they will choose the way of truth and set their hearts on Your laws.

Father God, I declare my children are the head and not the tail. They are above and not beneath. They will lend too many but will borrow from none. They will rule over many but none will rule over them. I have confidence that my children are blessed with the promises of Abraham.

Father God, I declare my children are more than conquerors. I am certain that in all things, You work for the good of those who love You.

Those who have been called according to Your purpose. I unshackle the plans of the Enemy from my children. I demand all bondages, soul ties, oppression, diseases, and all ungodly traits that my children's souls have put in place to be unchained. I give the Holy Spirit control over my children's minds, souls, bodies, and spirits.

In the precious name of Jesus I pray. Amen.

"The Spirit of the Sovereign LORD is upon me, for the LORD has anointed me to bring good news to the poor. He has sent me to comfort the brokenhearted and to proclaim that captives will be released and prisoners will be freed." (Isaiah 61:1 NLV)

Wisdom to Establish Guidelines and Rules

Heavenly Father, my desire is to parent my children in a fashion that is pleasing to You. Therefore, I submit myself to You completely. I realize I need Your help daily. I pray for Your gift of wisdom, discernment, revelation, guidance, patience, and strength. I pray the beauty of the Holy Spirit is so evident in me that I will be a good role model to my children.

Father God, I pray You will remove from me all things that hold me back from being the kind of parent You want me to be. Fill me with what I lack by equipping me with the ability, motivation insight, words, and commitment that I need to nurture my children. Show me how to love them unconditionally the same way You love me.

Holy Spirit, encourage me to faithfully intercede for my children. I pray that You will increase my awareness to sense the things that You put on my heart to pray about concerning their needs. Help me to obey God's Word and live right so my children will see my godly example. Bring me to my maturity, free me, heal me, and make me whole so that my stumbling blocks do not hinder the way I parent.

Father God, I pray that You will give me wisdom to establish rules and to implement them reasonably and consistently. Using fairness to apply guidelines and structure for both their good and bad behavior. I pray I will parent my children in such a manner that they will arise and call me blessed. I pray I will live a righteous life before them on the foundation of integrity so that my children are blessed after I am gone.

Father God, I made the choice to release my children into Your hands. I declare I am in partnership with You raising them. I leave all my worries with You. I know You care for them. I give You all the praise and all the glory for what You are doing in them. I have faith You will see them through to their completion.

In the precious name of Jesus I pray. Amen.

"The righteous lead blameless lives; blessed are their children after them." (Proverbs 20:7 NIV)

Leaving a Godly Legacy

Father God, I pray that the legacy that I leave my children will be a dedicated life and a pure heart before You. I pray I will remain faithful in my Christian walk by making the right choices. I believe no matter how impressive my achievements are there is nothing about my life that is worth remembering, with the acceptation of making a difference between eternal life and death in someone's life.

Holy Spirit, I desire to share my beliefs and the values that have been the keys to my spiritual growth with the next generation. Show me how to be a humble servant. Help me point my children to the Lord by emphasizing God's faithfulness and encouraging them to stay devoted to God. I pray You will help me finish well, to live a life of unconditional commitment and passion for Christ. I desire to live my life fully for God, leaving a godly legacy.

Father God, I refuse to live tied up to the past. I declare the past has no part in my life or the life of my children. I declare that Jesus has set us free. My children are delivered from the sinful ways that they have acquired from this world. I pray that my children will not become heirs to any ungodly earthly traits. I am certain when they trust in Jesus they will inherit Your kingdom, which You have prepared for them from the creation of this world.

Father God, I am confident that Jesus gave us power and authority over the Enemy. I take authority over all generational curses and any opposing influence from the past and present that are seeking after my children. I break them off right now by the power and authority given to me by Jesus. I pray specifically about (insert strong-holds here). I demand that these spirits flee from my children. I pray my children will reject everything that does not please You.

Father God, thank You that the old has passed away and the new has begun. I pray my children's lives are touched by my ministry and my sacrifices. I declare I will speak life over them. I will sow the seeds of Your unconditional love, Your dependable promises, kindness, hope, support, and positive words. Help me to teach my children about righteous things like faith, love, respect and charity.

Heavenly Father, I have faith the harvest will come, some while I am here and some after I have gone home to You. I pray the seed sown by my life will still be blooming and beautifying long after I have gone. I pray that the next generations will know You, even the children yet to be born.

In the precious name of Jesus I pray. Amen.

"So the next generation would know them, even the children yet to be born, they in turn would tell their children." (Psalm 78:6 NIV)

Surrender to the King

Heavenly Father, I am certain that every good and perfect gift is from above. Thank You for the precious children You have entrusted to me. They are truly a gift from You. I am convinced children born in one's youth are like arrows in the hands of a warrior, they are a reward and a heritage from You.

Father God, I realize You have placed these children in my hands. You have trusted me with them and You want me to take my role seriously. I believe You created each one of them for a particular purpose to have a specific impact on this world. I believe it is my role as their parent to seek Your will for understanding regarding the calling that are on my children. To train them up to be fully equipped to walk in those callings. I understand I cannot do this without You. That is why I surrender them into Your loving arms.

Holy Spirit, encourage me to pray continually about my children's needs and safety. Show me what to pray about and help me to trust that God knows what is best for them. I pray You will help me day after day to surrender my children into God's loving arms. I am certain when I start my children off on the way they should go, even when they are old, they will not turn from their path.

Father God, I am so grateful that Your angels surround my children and Your hedge of protection covers them and the blood of Jesus saves them. It is a comfort to know that You are always right by their sides, supporting them and giving them courage and strength.

Father God, I surrender my children into Your loving hands, from this day forward, they are Yours to keep. I realize that You know what is best for them. I have faith that You have already provided for all their needs. Thank You for giving them all the good things in life that can only come from You.

In the precious name of Jesus I pray. Amen.

"Children are a heritage from the Lord, offspring a reward from him. Like arrows in the hands of a warrior are children born in one's youth." (Psalm 127:3-4 NIV)

Releasing My Children into God's Hands

Father God, I present my children before You. I release them into Your hands. I lay them down at Your feet. I pray my children will humble themselves under Your mighty hand so that they will be exalted by You in due time. I pray they will not just listen to Your Word and deceive themselves but inspire them to do what Your Word commands.

Father God, I believe that You have come to call all sinners to repentance. I pray You will sanctify my children by Your truth. Help them to see that You love the world so much that You gave Your one and only son. I pray they will believe that whosoever trusts in Jesus shall not perish but will have everlasting life. I declare that my children shall confess that they have been crucified in Christ. I pray they will realize that they no longer live but that Jesus lives in them.

Lord Jesus, thank You for setting my children free. I pray they will rejoice in that freedom. I pray that believers who know Your Word will speak it faithfully to my children so they will grow in grace and knowledge.

Holy Spirit, encourage them to stand firm and not be burdened down by the yoke of slavery. Rather, let them clothe themselves with the Lord Jesus. I pray they will not think about how to gratify the desires of their sinful natures but will fix their eyes on Jesus, the author and finisher of their faith, so that they will not grow weary and lose heart.

Holy Spirit, I believe that a man's heart plans his way but that God directs his steps. I pray that my children will not be misled by bad company that will corrupt their good character. Give them revelation so they can cast off restraints. Guide them in the right way and lead them down an even path.

In the precious name of Jesus I pray. Amen.

"But grow in the grace and knowledge of our Lord and Savior Jesus Christ. To him be glory both now and forever! Amen." (2 Peter 3:18 NIV)

Patience to Parent with Love

Father God, I pray You will give me the patience to parent my children with love. I realize that patience does not develop overnight and I need Your power and goodness to development my patience. I know my patience is developed and strengthened by resting in Your perfect will and timing. I pray You will enable me to demonstrate the fruits of the spirit, the spiritual nature that produces love, joy, peace, patience, kindness, goodness, faithfulness, and self-control.

Father God, I pray You will show me how to express love to my children in a way that they will accept. I pray that You will help me to love them unconditionally as You love me. I desire to model Your love to them so that they will have no doubt of how strong my love is for them. I pray as my children come to understand the depths of Your love for them, they will also come to understand my love for them.

Heavenly Father, I pray my children will sense my love and they will understand that I am here for them. I pray that they will recognize that just because I don't agree with their point of view or I don't give them their way does not mean I don't love them.

Holy Spirit, I pray that when my child tests me, I will respond with wisdom. When I am irritable, I will show love and patience. When I am fixed in my own ways, You will teach me to be flexible. When I take myself too seriously, You will bless me with a sense of humor.

Father God, allow my children to grow each day and feel more and more loved by the people You have placed in their lives. I pray that their family members will demonstrate patience and love by accepting them the way that they are, looking past their rebellion and defiance. In Jesus' name, I command any feeling of rejection or condemnation that the Devil has planted in their minds to depart. I replace those feelings with a feeling of unconditional love and acceptance.

In the precious name of Jesus I pray. Amen.

"But the fruit of the Spirit is love, joy, peace, forbearance, kindness, goodness, faithfulness." (Galatians 5:22 NIV)

Fearfully and Wonderfully Made

Father God, thank You for placing Your grace and mercy on my children's lives. I believe You know everything about them. You know when they sit down and when they rise up. You are familiar with all their ways, even the very hairs on their heads You have numbered. I pray You will reveal to them that You think of them with thoughts of peace, not evil, a peace that passes all understanding, the peace that flows from the Cross of Calvary.

Father God, I am certain You determined the exact time of my children's births and where they would live. I declare they were made in Your image, and in You, my children live, move, and have their being because they are Your offspring. I have faith that You knew my children even before they were conceived. You knitted them together in the womb and brought them forth on the day they were born.

Heavenly Father, I have faith You will give my children extraordinary expected ends, that You have decreed and promised from the foundation of this world. I believe You chose them when You planned creation and their days are written in Your book. I declare they are fearfully and wonderfully made. I pray they will understand that Your thoughts for them are amazing, compassionate, and authoritative.

Heavenly Father, I am so grateful You are the complete expression of love. I believe it is Your desire to lavish Your love on my children simply because they are Your children and You are their Father. I am convinced You offer them more than an earthly father ever could because You are the perfect Father and every good and prefect gift that they obtain comes from Your hands.

Father God, I pray You will help my children to see that You are their provider and You meet all their needs. I have faith that Your plan for their future has always been filled with hope because You love them with an everlasting love. I am so grateful that Your thoughts toward my children are as countless as the grains of sand on the seashore and that You rejoice over them with singing. I have faith that You will never stop doing great things for them because they are Your treasured possessions.

In the precious name of Jesus I pray. Amen.

"I praise you because I am fearfully and wonderfully made; your works are wonderful, know that full well." (Psalm 139:14 NIV)

Plans for the Future

Father God, I pray my children will grow in the grace and knowledge of the Lord and Savior, Jesus Christ. I believe You have blessed them in the heavenly realm with every spiritual blessing in Christ Jesus. I am confident that You hold their world in Your hands and Your plans for them are better than anything they could have ever hoped for or imagined.

Father God, I pray that You will guide my children in the direction that You have designed for them. I am certain that You have called all sinners to repentance and that a man's heart plans his own ways but that You direct his steps. I have confidence You will instruct them in

Your ways and lead them down smooth paths. I am certain when they call upon You and pray to You, You will listen to them. When they seek You with all their hearts, they will find You.

Heavenly Father, I believe You have perfect plans for my children's futures. Plans that You have tailored just for them and those plans complement the things You are building into their characters right now. Help them to realize the plans You have for them are not the same as Your plans for their friends. Show them that all of their experiences, both good and bad, fit into Your plans and are part of Your ideal design for them. I pray my children will humble themselves under Your mighty hand so that they can be exalted by You in due time.

Holy Spirit, I pray that my children will not be anxious about anything but in every situation; they will present their needs before God, while offering thanksgiving. I pray my children will live as Jesus did and stop thinking about satisfying the desires of their sinful nature. Encourage them to understand that Christ has freed them so that they may enjoy the benefits of freedom. I pray that they will become firm in this freedom and will not become slaves again.

In the precious name of Jesus I pray. Amen.

"Do not be anxious about anything, but in every situation, by prayer and petition, with thanksgiving, present your requests to God." (Philippians 4:6 NIV)

Ability to Produce Wealth

Father God, thank You for satisfying my children's every need in a glorious way through Christ Jesus. I pray You will open their eyes to see that it is You who gives them the ability to generate wealth. I declare You are their Jehovah Jireh and You provide for all of their needs. I pray that my children will spend their money wisely and give generously towards Your kingdom's cause.

Father God, I pray that all my children's accomplishments are pleasing to You and their achievements line up with Your will. I pray that my children will find favor in Your sight. I have faith that above all things, You wish for them to prosper and be in good health, even as their souls prosper. I pray that they will not be fixated on what they think they don't have and miss the unexpected ways You meet those very needs. I believe that You know all their struggles and You are working to help them flourish, even when they can't see it.

Holy Spirit, encourage my children to commit their plans and ventures to God. I believe He will help them succeed when they are in His will. I have confidence He will increase their greatness and comfort them on each side. I declare that my children are the head, they are above. They are blessed when they come in and when they go out because God has established His covenant with them.

Father God, I take comfort in knowing that Your promises remain the same yesterday, today, and forever. I am convinced that the words that come from Your mouth will not come back to You without results but Your words will accomplish whatever You desire and achieve whatever You send Your Word to do.

In the precious name of Jesus I pray. Amen.

"My word, which comes from my mouth, is like the rain and snow. It will not come back to me without results. It will accomplish whatever I want and achieve whatever I send it to do." (Isaiah 55:11 GW)

Deliverance through the Valley

Father God, I declare that You are my children's shepherd and they shall not want. You cause them to lie down in green pasture and You lead them beside quiet waters. You have restored their souls. You guide them in the path of righteousness for Your namesake. Although they may walk through the valley of the shadow of death, they will fear no evil because Your rod and Your staff comfort them.

Father God, I declare You have prepared a table before my children in the presence of their enemies. You have anointed their heads with oil and their cups overflow. Surely, goodness and love will follow them all the days of their lives, and they will dwell in the house of the Lord forever.

Father God, I declare that my children will serve You forever. I pray that You will call my children Your own. Reveal to them the spiritual truths that define whose they are and who they are. Open their eyes to see that when they come to Christ, You do more than save them from an eternity apart from You. Reveal to them that You saved them for Your purpose, not their own purpose. Show them when You are the Lord of their lives, they cannot fail and they will not lack anything in life.

Holy Spirit, I pray You will reveal to my children when they obey God's commandments, blessing will come. I pray You will give them the courage and the strength to understand that with God, they have deliverance through the valley because they are more than conquerors through Christ Jesus.

In the precious name of Jesus I pray. Amen.

The Lord is My Shepherd: (Psalm 23 NIV)

Lighting Their Path

Heavenly Father, I have confidence my children will find You when they seek You with their whole hearts. I declare that Your Word is a lamp for their feet and a light for their path. I am certain that You know the plans that You have for them, plans to give them hope and a future. I pray that they will not just be believers in Christ but that they will be followers. I have faith that You instruct, guide, and protect those who follow You.

Holy Spirit, I pray You will teach my children to do God's will and give them the strength to achieve it. Guide them down a safe path and lead them in the ways that they should go. I have faith when they wander off the road to the left or to the right; they will hear Your voice behind them saying, "This is the way. Follow me." I am confident they will hear clear answers from God in all areas of their lives.

Holy Spirit, I pray You will light my children's path with love and that Jesus' light will be their morning star. I pray as they journey through life and come to dark crossroads that seem challenging, and when they cannot see the light at the end; they will remember that when they follow Jesus, their darkened paths will meet up with the bright path God planned for them all along.

Father God, I pray that You will give my children ears to hear You and eyes to see You. I pray You will open their eyes to see Your vision and open their ears to hear Your voice. I am confident that You lead the blind on unfamiliar paths and You turn their darkness into light in front of them. You make rough places smooth and You will never abandon them.

In the precious name of Jesus I pray. Amen.

"Your word is a lamp for my feet, a light on my path." (Psalm 119:105 NIV)

Receiving the Joy of the Lord

Gracious Heavenly Father, I pray that my children will be filled with the joy of the Holy Spirit and that joy will rise up in their souls. I am confident they will discover that true love, joy, and happiness are in Your presence. Open their eyes to see that they lose joy by grieving the Holy Spirit, and when that happens, they become separated from their source of true joy, and peace. Reveal to them that the Holy Spirit is grieved when they no longer submit humbly in obedience to Your will.

Holy Spirit, encourage my children to obey the Lord and come before Him with joyful singing. Remind them that even though they will face trouble and trials during this life, hardship will always be followed by peace and restoration because the joy of the Lord is their strength. I pray they will joyfully sing about their victories and they will wave their flags of triumph in God's name.

Father God, I take hold of my authority over the Devil. I demand him to release my children. I break the power of any negative emotions that are surrounding them. I declare that this is the day that the Lord has made and they will rejoice and be glad in it. I proclaim that negative attitudes have no place in their minds. I pray when negative thoughts do come, the Holy Spirit will comfort them and give them the peace that surpasses all understanding.

Father God, I speak joy, peace, comfort, encouragement, love, and contentment over my children. I pray that they will rejoice in their salvation because the truth has set them free. I have faith that whomever the Son sets free is free indeed. I pray my children will shout joyfully about You and they will serve You with gladness.

Holy Spirit, I pray my children will see that no matter what temporary situation they are in, their faith in God's salvation is an endless reason for joy and thanksgiving. Reveal to them that the knowledge of their salvation sets them free from their past and gives them faith for the present and glorious hope for the future.

In the precious name of Jesus I pray. Amen.

"May we shout for joy over your victory and lift up our banners in the name of our God. May the Lord grant all your requests." (Psalm 20:5 NIV)

Sheltered and Protected

Holy Spirit, I declare that my children dwell in the shelter of the Most High. They find rest in the shadow of the Almighty because God is their refuge and their fortress, the only God in whom they can trust. I am certain He will save them from the Enemies snare and from all deadly disease. I have faith He will cover them with His feathers and that under His wings, they will find refuge.

Father God, I am certain Your faithfulness is their shield and barricade, so my children will not fear the terror of night, or the arrow that fly by day, or the deadly disease that stalks in the darkness, or the plague that destroys at midday. I declare a thousand may fall at their sides and ten thousand at their right hands, but it will not come near them. They will only observe with their eyes and see the punishment of the wicked.

Father God, I declare You are my children's refuge and their dwelling place and no harm will overtake them and no disaster will come near their homes. I have faith You will command Your angels to guard them in all their ways. Your angels will lift them up in their hands so that they will not strike their feet against a stone. I declare my children will tread on the lion and the cobra. They will trample the great lion and the serpent.

Father God, I have faith that when my children choose to love You. You will rescue them and You will protect them because they acknowledge Your name. When they call on You, You will answer them. I am confident You will be with them in trouble. You will deliver them and honor them with long life. You will satisfy them and show them their salvation.

In the precious name of Jesus I pray. Amen.

The Shadow of the Almighty: (Psalm 91:1-16)

Deliver My Children from Evil

Heavenly Father, I am so thankful for the good work You have begun in my children. I have absolute faith that You will carry it on to completion. I pray You will equip them with all that they need to do Your will. I have faith You will accomplish Your good and perfect plan in them and they will become spiritually mature. I pray that the words of their mouths and the mediation of their hearts will be acceptable in Your sight.

Holy Spirit, I pray my children will come to their repentance and they will listen and believe God's every word while they are young. I pray You will influence their hearts and open their ears to hear God's voice and open their eyes to see His glory. Reach into their hearts and pull out all darkness so that God's glorious light can shine inside. Fill them with Your presence and give them a holy hatred for sin.

Lord Jesus, I pray they will see all their sins through the Cross of Calvary. I pray they will recall all their un-confessed sins and they will repent from them. Provide them with the strength and courage to confess their sins and help them to turn away from their mistakes. I pray that You will cleanse their hearts and their thoughts and put a shield upon their faith that the Devil cannot penetrate.

Father God, I pray You will rest Your mighty and powerful hand on my children, pulling down all strongholds, addictions, habits, or everything that attempts to exalt itself against You or in place of the knowledge of You. I pray that You will strengthen my children and protect them from all harm. I pray that You will rescue them from the hands of their enemies and that You will deliver them from the evil of the wicked men of this world.

Father God, I believe You will protect my children. I am so grateful that our spiritual weapons are mighty and the authority given to us by Jesus is far greater and above the Devil so that the Enemy must yield. I am confident that with You, all things are possible. I have faith that the works of the Enemy will be torn down.

Lord Jesus, I take my authority; through the power given to me by Your shed blood. In Your name, I speak to the Devil. Satan I command you to release my children. You no longer have any control over their thoughts, actions, conduct, feelings, or any part of their lives. I command all ancestral curses that are against my children be released. I command the Enemy to yield, stop, cease, and halt in all activities in my children's lives.

In the precious name of Jesus I pray. Amen.

"Being confident of this, that he who began a good work in you will carry it on to completion until the day of Christ Jesus." (Philippians 1:6 NIV)

Seeking after God

Dear Heavenly Father, I pray my children will seek You with all their hearts. I am confident when they seek You with all their hearts they will find You. I believe that You desire to establish great and marvelous things in them. I declare when they delight in You, You will give them the desires of their hearts because it is You who creates those desires.

Father God, I trust You are able to do more for my children than they can possibly imagine because You are their greatest encourager. You are also the one who comforts them in all their troubles. I am certain when my children are brokenhearted, You are close to them. As a shepherd carries a lamb, You carry them close to Your heart. I am grateful that one day, You will wipe away every tear from their eyes and take away all the pain they have suffered on this earth.

Father God, I am convinced You are their heavenly Father and You love them even as You love Jesus and in Jesus; Your love for them is revealed. I believe that Jesus is the exact likeness of You. I am certain that Jesus came to demonstrate that You are for my children, not against them. He came to tell them You are not counting their fault and wrongdoing. I believe Jesus died so they could be reconciled with You. His death is the ultimate expression of Your love for them. Thank You for giving up everything You loved so they might gain Your love.

Lord Jesus, I pray that my children will pursue and trust in You. I pray they will receive the gift of salvation that You give so freely. I have faith when they do, nothing will ever separate them from Your love. Thank You for the precious blood You shed that covers all their sins and the sacrifice You made so that they could have eternal life.

In the precious name of Jesus I pray. Amen.

"But from there you will seek the Lord your God, and you will find Him if you search for Him with all your heart and all your soul." (Deuteronomy 4:29 NASB)

Achieving a Teachable Spirit

Father God, I pray my children will never be so careless to turn away from Your teachings. I pray they will seek the knowledge of Your Word and they will choose to keep a teachable attitude. I am certain You admire those who are teachable, those who listen and chase after wisdom. I pray that they will want to obtain wisdom and knowledge. Above all, they will listen to Your instructions and spend time in Your Word every day.

Heavenly Father, I am convinced when my children have the knowledge of You, they find integrity and certainty. I declare the fear of the Lord brings knowledge and peace. I have faith that my children can accomplish anything they put their attention to and they can be taught lifelong relationship skills, academic lessons, and spiritual truth that they will need.

Holy Spirit, I pray You will instill in my children understanding so that learning will come to them effortlessly. I pray You will motivate them to obtain knowledge and they will find joy in the process of reading and learning. I pray that they will take the skills, abilities, and talents they have been blessed with and use them for Your kingdom's cause. I pray You will handpick the people who will influence them spiritually, academically, and intelligently. I pray You will give them God-ordained favor with family, friends, teachers, instructors, and bosses.

Father God, I pray that my children will achieve and increase in outstanding communication skills and that they will have the desire to be excellent in all their work. I have confidence You have already given them clear minds so that they can easily comprehend what they learn. I pray that the clarity of their minds allows them to adequately memorize, organize, and express what they have learned.

Father God, I have confidence when my children apply their hearts to instruction and their ears to the way of knowledge, You will impart to them understanding in all things. I pray they will have the desire to learn, read, teach, and preach Your Word. I pray they give You all the praise and glory for the wisdom You have established in them.

In the precious name of Jesus I pray. Amen.

"Apply your heart to instruction and your ears to words of knowledge." (Proverbs 23:12 NIV)

Praise from Their Lips

Heavenly Father, I am certain that from the lips of children and infants, You have ordained praise. I pray that my children will always exalt You at all times and their lips will overflow with praise as they learn Your commands. I pray that at a young age my children will come to You and no one will hinder them. I am convinced the kingdom of heaven belongs to those who are like little children.

Holy Spirit, encourage my children to look up to the God that created them. I pray that the hand that has made them will protect them from their enemies. I have certainty that through the praise of children and infants, God has established a stronghold against all of His enemies to silence the Enemy and the Avenger.

Heavenly Father, I pray that my children will listen to Your instructions and they will not forsake Your teachings. I declare that my children will continually offer to You a sacrifice of praise with the fruit of their lips and in doing this they will increase in knowledge and happiness for all eternity. I pray that each new degree of knowledge they find regarding You will excite an equal desire to praise You.

In the precious name of Jesus I pray. Amen.

"Through the praise of children and infants you have established a stronghold against your enemies, to silence the foe and the avenger." (Psalm 8:2 NIV)

Rejoicing in God's Good Design

Father God, I pray my children will rejoice in You always. I pray they will see their purpose and acknowledge who they are in Christ. I pray they will recognize and accept what Jesus has done for them, and they will act, and live out their relationships and redemption by being obedient to Your will.

Heavenly Father, I declare my children will possess a pursuit for You. As a result, You will become the driving force, inspiration, motivation, and reason for all they do in life. I am confident that pursuing You will bring a true happiness they can rejoice in forever. I pray my children will love You with all that is within them. I have confidence You will saturate them with the peace that they need, Your peace that passes all understanding.

Holy Spirit, inspire my children to rejoice. Help them to see that God created them in His good design and in His image. I declare my children are God's workmanship, created in Christ Jesus to do the good work that was prepared in advance for them.

Father God, I pray You will use my children mightily for Your kingdom. Give them God-ordained encounters and ministry positions that You have predestined for them before the foundation of this world. I pray that my children will find promotion first with You and then with men. Please open doors of opportunity for them that no man can shut. I pray You will encourage them to look ahead and not behind. Give my children dreams, visions, and discernment.

Father God, I pray that every word that comes out of their mouths is acceptable in Your sight. I pray their words, actions, and conduct give You glory. I declare that health, happiness, and prosperity belong to them, and they are wonderfully blessed and highly favored. I proclaim that my children are born-again and baptized in the Holy Spirit. I declare this is the day that the Lord has made and my children will rejoice and be glad in it.

In the precious name of Jesus I pray. Amen.

"Always be joyful in the Lord! I'll say it again: Be joyful." (Philippians 4:4 GW)

Hungering and Thirsting for God

Heavenly Father, I pray that my children will hunger for Your touch, thirst for Your presence, love to spend time with You in prayer, praise, and worship. I pray they will thirst for Your Word like a newborn baby cries for milk. I pray they will want to be in Your Word and in Your house every moment they can. I declare my children will seek after Your truth, be led by the Holy Spirit, and have faith and courage to do what You tell them to do. I pray they will hear Your voice and their strength will be renewed and refreshed daily.

Father God, I pray You will remove from my children's hearts any distractions that are keeping them from You. I pray that ungodliness and all that opposes You, will disgust them and they will be drawn to things that are full of Your love and light. I pray that they will fear You and that they will depart from all evil. I pray they will comprehend there are consequences to their choices and actions. I pray that they understand they have the choice of life and death. I pray they will grasp that living for their flesh and worldly things will cause spiritual death.

Holy Spirit, I pray You will give my children teachable spirits. Remove from them the attitude of "I know it all" and replace it with a mindset of "I want to learn." I declare they are set free from pride, laziness, and self-gratification. I pray that my children will say yes to the things of God and no to the things of the flesh.

Father God, I pray that every choice that my children make will be overflowing with love and reverence towards You. Write Your laws upon their hearts so that they will walk with confidence and assurance of the righteousness of Your commands. I pray that they will become prayer warriors, and that they will call upon You passionately, and listen to You in silence. Help them to see that man does not live on bread alone but on every word that comes from Your mouth. I pray that their daily walks with You will glow with the Holy Spirit's presence and they will have an unwavering hunger for praiseworthy things.

In the precious name of Jesus I pray Amen.

"He humbled you, causing you to hunger and then feeding you with manna, which neither you nor your ancestors had known, to teach you that man does not live on bread alone but on every word that comes from the mouth of the Lord." (Deuteronomy 8:3 NIV)

Called According to His Purpose

Father God, I believe my children are called according to Your purpose because You have spoken their names and brought them to their salvation. I have faith You have positioned them where they are so You can bring about Your purpose. I pray You will give them the strength they need to accomplish Your plans. Equip them with strong faith so that they can walk blamelessly in Your sight.

Heavenly Father, I have faith that there is absolutely no limit to what You can accomplish through my children when they trust in Your power and grace. I believe that with You, all things are possible. I am completely convinced that all things work together for those who love You. Who have been called according to Your purpose.

Father God, I pray when my children are displaying purposeless and rebellious behavior, You will capture their hearts. I am confident that You are the potter and they are Your clay. I pray You will make and mold them into the image of Jesus. I have faith that You will make them into new creations and complete in them the good works that You have already started.

Holy Spirit, give my children the understanding of God's unfailing faithfulness and love. Speak to their hearts and reveal to them God's forgiveness, tender grace, and infallible Word. Give them ears to hear God's quiet whisper and eyes to see His glory.

Heavenly Father, I pray that the desires and passions of my children's hearts line up with Your purpose for them. I am certain that knowing Your purpose for their lives is one of the best things they could ever discover. I am convinced we are called to bring glory to You on this earth and the way we do this is by completing the work You have prearranged for us. I pray You will help them understand the assignments they are meant to carry out for You.

Father God, I lay my children at Your feet. I place them into Your everlasting arms. I pray You will carry them under Your wings, keeping them close to Your heart protecting them from their enemies so they can complete the purpose You have for them. I come before You with confidence, believing in Your Word and trusting in Your promises. I am confident You will turn Your ears to me and answer my prayers because I place all my hope in You. I have faith that before long my children will realize the purposes You have placed in them.

In the precious name of Jesus I pray Amen.

"And we know that in all things God works for the good of those who love him, who have been called according to his purpose." (Romans 8:28 NIV)

Unlimited Encouragement

Heavenly Father, I am thankful You offer my children the privilege to experience Your grace through the forgiveness of sins. I have faith that in Jesus, they have received redemption through His blood and the forgiveness of sins in unity with the riches of Your grace. I am certain that because my children have been justified through faith, they have peace and encouragement with You through Jesus.

Father God, I am so grateful that my children's relationship with You is not based on their performance or good works but on their faith. I am certain that Jesus is the way, the truth, and the life and that no one can come to You except through Jesus. As a result, there is no condemnation toward those who are in Christ Jesus.

Holy Spirit, I am confident You are my children's greatest encourager and You are also the one who comforts them in all their troubles. I pray You will encourage their hearts and strengthen them in every good deed and word. I declare I will also encourage my children and their walks of faith so that my words will minister grace to them.

Father God, I believe You hear the petition of the afflicted and You encourage them and listen to their cries. I trust in Your grace, that restored and redeemed my children. I am so grateful that the Lord Jesus Christ Himself loves them and His grace and mercy offers them unlimited encouragement and awe-inspiring hope.

In the precious name of Jesus I pray Amen.

"You, Lord, hear the desire of the afflicted; you encourage them, and you listen to their cry." (Psalm 10:17 NIV)

Faith in Jesus

Father God, I pray that my children will have the faith to love You with their whole minds, whole hearts, and whole souls and that they will have the peace they need, Your peace, which surpasses all understanding. I am certain when they fix their eyes on Jesus, the author and finisher of their faith, they will not grow weary and lose heart but will be strengthened by Your Word.

Holy Spirit, I pray my children will reach their destination with complete assurance in their faith. Persuade them to continue to draw near to God with a sincere heart and strong faith. Encourage them to stand strong, holding firmly to their declaration of faith with certainty that the one who made the promise is faithful.

Gracious Father, help my children to see that when they have faith in Jesus. They don't just receive forgiveness of sins, but they are raised up with Jesus to share in His place of honor. I pray they will understand that the power of life and death is in their tongues and they need to verbally declare their faith. I pray my children will confess that they have been crucified with Christ and that they no longer live but that Christ lives in them. I am grateful my children shall rejoice because their names are written in the book of life.

Father God, I am confident You will reveal to my children that You have called them to persevere. Give them revelation so they can cast off restraints. Help them to be on their guard and stand firm in their faith, to be courageous and strong. Teach them to appreciate that Christ is their living hope, and that Your grace, and abundant mercy is available to them both now, and as an inheritance to come.

Heavenly Father, reveal to my children that by faith in Christ, ordinary people became extraordinary and leave behind an everlasting legacy, reputation, and example that others can follow. Show them that they are not alone in this journey of faith but that they have a great multitude of witnesses in those who have gone before them and upon whose shoulders they can stand.

In the precious name of Jesus I pray. Amen.

"Fixing our eyes on Jesus, the pioneer and perfector of faith. For the joy set before him he endured the cross, scorning its shame, and sat down at the right hand of the throne of God." (Hebrews 12:2 NIV)

Freedom from Ungodly Strongholds

Dear Lord, I believe in Your Word, and I trust in Your promises. I have faith You have promised to deliver us when we cry out to You for help. I ask for Your deliverance, and I cry out to You on the behalf of my children. I am confident You will contend with those who contend with me and my children shall be saved.

Father God, I realize my children walk in the flesh, but they do not war according to the flesh. I proclaim their weapons of warfare are not material but are mighty and divine for pulling down strongholds and casting down arguments or everything that exalts itself against the knowledge of You. I pray that You will deliver my children from any and all ungodliness that is trying to take root in them. I pray that You will work deliverance in them wherever it is needed. I pray that my children will live by Your commands and they will not gratify the desires of their sinful nature.

Father God, I have faith You will guide, protect, cover, and correct my children when sin is trying to take root or when evil is trying to place strongholds on them. I pray You will give them the wisdom and strength to fight. I pray that they will learn to run to You in times of troubles. I declare that You are their shield and their strength. I have faith that You will deliver them from every evil attack and preserve them for Your heavenly kingdom.

Father God Almighty, thank You for standing beside me in the spiritual battle for my children, I can not do it without Your guidance. I place them in Your mighty arms. I have faith that Your hand will always be upon them. Grant me wisdom and revelation of what to pray for concerning their strongholds. Let all that is hidden come to light. If there are any actions I need to take, please show me and help me accomplish them.

In the precious name of Jesus I pray. Amen.

"I look for Your deliverance, Lord." (Genesis 49:18 NIV)

Abstaining from Premarital Sex

Father God, I pray that my children will live by Your commands and have healthy relationships. Help them to feel about sexuality as You designed it to be. Help them to see that a relaxed attitude about sex robs them of its God-given beauty. Reveal to them that now is the time to set high standards about sexual behavior before marriage. I pray they will comprehend that they have a gift that is too precious to open early. I pray that they will not play on the edge or see how far they can go with premarital sex. Instead, let purity be their goal.

Father God, I pray that my children will realize that sex before marriage is not a good idea. Reveal to them that the fire they think they can control will burn out of control and that premarital sex will do more damage than they could ever have anticipated. Reveal to my children that sex is intended for marriage and that sex outside of marriage will never give them the unconditional love they require. Help them realize that sex outside of marriage is always a mistake.

Holy Spirit, I pray that when my children are tempted to cross the line to premarital sexual behavior, You will provide them with the strength and wisdom to say no. Guard them from lust and temptation, and if they fall into sexual sin, may their hearts not be torn apart by it. I pray if they have crossed the line into premarital sexual behavior that You will begin to restore their spiritual and emotional integrity.

Father God, encourage them to set examples for others in their behavior, in friendships, and in purity. I pray that homosexuality will never be a thought in their minds. Keep them away from the presence of any evil. Show my children that whoever desires to be friends to this world makes themselves an enemy to You.

In the precious name of Jesus, I pray. Amen.

"Don't let anyone look down on you because you are young, but set an example for the believers in speech, in conduct, in love, in faith and in purity." (1 Timothy 4:12 NIV)

Take Every Thought Captive

Father God, I pray You will take captive my children's every thought to make it obedient to Christ. Help them to see that they have the authority to cast down and demolish every argument and every charade that sets itself up against the knowledge of You. I pray they will take authority over every one of their thoughts that does not conform to Your standards.

Father God, encourage my children to evaluate all of their thoughts, desires, and behaviors. Inspire them to bring everything under the control of Jesus. Help them realize that compared to the mind of Christ, their abilities of reasoning are insignificant and trivial. I pray You will reveal to my children that You know their every thought. Help them to recognize that Your thoughts are beyond the understanding of our human minds.

Holy Spirit, convince my children to examine their hearts and minds. Help them identify their true desires and motives. Provide them with the help that they need to become Christ like. Help them to see that the ways that God thinks and reasons are superior to anything our minds can grasp. Reveal to them that God's ways are much higher than ours and infinitely more trustworthy.

Father God, I declare victory, peace, wholeness, and healing for my children because they are Your workmanship, created in Christ Jesus to do the good works that You prepared in advance for them. I take comfort in knowing that You are in control and You know the beginning from the end.

In the precious name of Jesus, I pray. Amen.

"We demolish arguments and every pretension that sets itself up against the knowledge of God, and we take captive every thought to make it obedient to Christ." (2 Corinthians 10:5 NIV)

Exercising Spiritual Weapons

Heavenly Father, thank You for the privilege to exercise the spiritual weapons You have given us. I believe the weapons we use in our fight are not made by humans. Rather, they are powerful weapons from You. With those spiritual weapons we can destroy people's defenses and arguments. In the name of Your one and only Son, Jesus Christ, my Lord and Savior. I command all spirits that are not the Holy Spirit to depart from my children.

Lord Jesus, in Your precious name, I command the spirit of hatred, worry, torment, idleness, deceit, discontentment, insensitivity, death, disorder, arrogance, dishonor, ungratefulness, poverty, discord, corruption, wickedness, failure, strongholds, evil, dishonesty, disobedient, weakness, low self-esteem, doubt, discouragement, sickness, division and any and all ungodly spirits not mentioned by name depart from my children, never to return again.

Father God, I am confident that every good and perfect gift comes from You. I speak blessing over my children. I declare over my children love, peace, joy, energy, truth, contentment, kindness, life, unity, humility, honor, thankfulness, wealth, harmony, integrity, righteousness, success, victory, godliness, honest, obedience, strength, high self-esteem, hope, encouragement, health, restoration, freedom, mercy, grace, angels, and the power of the Holy Spirit.

Father God, I proclaim that the blood of Jesus protects and covers my children souls, minds, spirits, and bodies. I pray that You will release Your warrior angels to surround them wherever they go. I am certain that Your hedge of protection will guard and cover them, their homes, and everything that affect them.

In the precious name of Jesus I pray. Amen.

"The weapons we use in our fight are not made by humans. Rather, they are powerful weapons from God. With them we destroy people's defenses, that is, their arguments." (2 Corinthians 10:4 GW)

Enjoying a Life of Healing and Health

Dear Heavenly Father, I am thankful that You answer prayers and when Your children are in trouble, all we need to do is call on You and You will rescue us. I have faith we do not need to worry about anything, but in every situation, we should let You know what we need in prayer while we give thanks.

Father God, I am convinced that You give strength to the weary and increase the power of the weak. I pray for my children's physical, emotional, and spiritual healing. I have faith You are the healer of the brokenhearted. You are the one who bandages our wounds. I am confident that You will give them power when they are weak. When they have no might, You will increase their strength.

Holy Spirit, encourage my children to wait upon the Lord. Help them understand that their faith in God assures them of the things they expect and convinces them of the things they cannot see. I declare God is their shield and refuge, their ever-present help in times of trouble. I have faith before they call, God will answer. While they are still speaking, He hears and comes to their rescue. I pray that my children will wait patiently, so they can renew their strength and they will be able to run and not grow weary, and walk and not be faint.

Lord Jesus, I pray You will rebuke the Devourer and demolish all strongholds placed on my children. Annihilate all curses that have been made against them from affecting them in any way. I am confident that You bore the stripes on Your back for all sin and by those stripes, Your followers are healed. I claim supernatural health and well-being over my children. I declare because of the precious blood that You shed my children are healed and whole.

Father God, I am grateful that our spiritual weapons are mighty and the authority of Jesus is far greater than the power of darkness, so the Enemy must yield. In the name of Your one and only Son, Jesus Christ, my Lord and Savior, I command all spirits of poor health to depart from my children. I command that the yoke of sickness, aches, disease, syndromes, disorders, conditions and infections be destroyed.

In the precious name of Jesus I pray. Amen.

"He gives strength to the weary and increases the power of the weak." (Isaiah 40:29 NIV)

Staying Attracted to Holiness and Purity

Gracious Heavenly Father, I pray that You will saturate my children with Your love, which surpasses all understanding. I pray that the love they have for You is stronger than their love for anyone or anything else. I am confident when Your Word is hidden in their hearts sin must flee from them. Strengthen them to only be attracted to holiness and purity and give them the courage to run from ungodly or evil things.

Holy Spirit, teach my children to respect and understand God's laws and recognize that His laws are for their benefit. Help them to see that when they do not follow His ways, their lives will end up in chaos. Encourage them to set examples for others in their speech, behavior, and faithfulness. Enable them to do what is pure and holy.

Father God, I pray You will whisper into my children's hearts and surround them with songs of victory. Purify their characters and thoughts. Give them the revelation that living in purity brings life, holiness, and blessings. I pray my children will understand that the greatest reward is satisfying You.

Lord Jesus, I am certain that blessed are the pure in heart, for they shall see God. I pray my children's hearts are purified, their motives are holy, and their reflections are of You. I pray that the clothes that they wear, the way that they speak, the music that they listen to, and the places they go will display a reverence and desire to exalt You. I am certain when they choose to look for You with all their hearts, they will find You.

In the precious name of Jesus I pray. Amen.

"Don't let anyone look down on you for being young. Instead, make your speech, behavior, love, faith, and purity an example for other believers." (1 Timothy 4:12 GW)

Steering Clear of Alcohol, Drugs, and Other Addictions

Heavenly Father, I pray that my children will have the discernment to say no to anything that leads to death and yes to things that lead to life. I pray they will choose life and truth in every decision they make. I declare their only dependency is Jesus and they are delivered from all evil. I pray that You will steer my children clear from all addictions, especially cigarettes, alcohol, drugs, pornography, and evil of any kind.

Holy Spirit, stop my children if they try anything that is harmful to their health, bodies, minds, or souls. I pray they will allow You to take control. Teach my children to resist all sinful temptations and encourage them to claim the victory that Jesus Christ won over Satan when He died on the Cross and rose again.

Lord Jesus, thank You for giving Your followers the authority over all the power of the Enemy, so that we can walk among snakes and scorpions and crush them under our feet. I am certain nothing will injure us. I am grateful for the divine power that I can use to demolish all strongholds. I take authority with that divine power and I put a stop to all the plans that the Devil has to devastate, destroy, influence and addict my children.

Lord Jesus, in Your name, I command all spirits of addictions to come to an end this very moment. I take authority over any generational curses on my children; anything that is in them that would lead them toward destructive behavior. I break all ancestral curses that have been passed down from either side of their families. I command Satan to release my children from all strongholds that he has placed on them.

Father God, I pray that my children will realize and confess that their bodies are the Holy Spirit's temple. I pray their choices, decisions, and habits will bring You glory. I proclaim they are under the blood covenant of Jesus. I pray You will place a hedge of protection around my children. I ask that Your warrior angels cover them under their wings.

In the precious name of Jesus I pray. Amen.

"Look, I have given you authority over all the power of the enemy and you can walk among snakes and scorpions and crush them. Nothing will injure you." (2 Corinthians 10:4 NIV)

Feeling a Sense of Worth

Father God, I am so grateful that my children are the apple of Your eye and You hide them in the shadow of Your wings. I pray You will open their hearts to see that Jesus is the one person with whom they are totally safe and who they can completely trust. I pray that my children will feel and accept Your love. Give them strong self-esteem, yet teach them to be humble. Flood their hearts with Your never-ending love and contentment.

Father God, I pray You will reveal to my children that You know all about them and You accept and love them just as they are. Reveal to them You will not leave them or forsake them. Help them to see all their abilities, experiences, battles, weaknesses, and strengths are all a divine tapestry to make them instruments to accomplish everything they are here to achieve.

Holy Spirit, encourage my children to abide in the love of Jesus. Help them realize that God loves them so much that He sent His one and only Son to die for them. I pray You will reveal to my children that humbleness is the secret of self-worth. Show them that humility is always teachable, gentle, thankful, considerate, and willing to accept responsibility rather than place blame.

Lord Jesus, I pray that You will deliver my children from all the lies that the Devil has spoken against them. In Your name, I demand all curses that have been spoken against my children to depart. I pray they will release all doubt and unworthiness from their minds and they will recognize that their self-worth comes from You.

Father God, I pray my children will experience Your loving kindness in the morning and will hear Your soft whisper in the evening. Let them feel Your never-ending love penetrate their hearts so that their souls will be satisfied. I declare that they are blessed with the awesome gift of love that You give so generously. I pray they will come to a place where they decide to trust in You at all times.

In the precious name of Jesus I pray. Amen.

"Keep me as the apple of your eye; hide me in the shadow of your wings." (Psalm 17:8 NIV)

Resisting Rebellion

Father God, I completely surrender my rebellious children to You. I have faith You hear their every cry and know all their thoughts, ideas, regrets, fears, and rebellious behavior. I am confident You can change their hearts, minds, and actions. I have faith by the works of the Cross of Calvary; You have already set them free. I am certain whosoever the Son sets free are free indeed.

Father God, I pray that my children will confess and repent from all the sins they have committed against You. I am confident You will cleanse and forgive all their rebelliousness. I pray that they will desire to obey You as their heavenly Father, me as their parent, and the people in authority that You have placed over them.

Holy Spirit, help my children not to give themselves over to pride, selfishness, and rebellion. I pray You will rescue them from all that is not within God's will. I pray they will feel embarrassed and uncomfortable with misbehavior, disobedience, and worldly things.

Lord Jesus, I take authority in Your name, and I stand against the schemes of the Devil. I declare that all the rebellion that my children are displaying will come to an end today. I command that all spirits of rebellion must depart from my children. I terminate the spirit of idolatry, rebellion, stubbornness, hostility, and disrespect. They will have no part in their lives. I declare my children will not walk in the path of death or destruction.

Father God, I pray You will encourage my children to have respect, and obedience toward authority, toward You, and toward their family members so that their lives will be long and excellent. I pray You will establish in them sweet and humble hearts and they will walk in obedience.

In the precious name of Jesus I pray. Amen.

"I will cleanse them from all the sin they have committed against me and will forgive all their sins of rebellion against me." (Jeremiah 33:8 NIV)

CHAPTER 4

Praying for Loved Ones

It is the will of God for all to be saved and come to the knowledge of His truth, and our prayers can be an authoritative force in the lives of our unsaved family and friends. God is faithful to hear our prayers. Even if our words are not impressive, we should trust Him and say what is in our hearts concerning our loved ones and have confidence that God has the ability to strengthen, restore, heal, and deliver them.

As Christians, we are called to pray without ceasing, and we need to learn how to pray according to the wisdom and Word of God. It is my prayer for Jesus to abide in my loved ones' hearts and for them to feel the freedom that He gives through salvation so that they will be rooted, and grounded in God's love, and are able to understand the extent of His love. I am convinced that God wants to open their eyes in order that they can see Him clearly, and open their hearts so they can know Him intimately, and open their minds so that they can understand the Scriptures.

It is time for us to realize that we are not in a battle with flesh and blood but that we are contending against demonic powers and wicked spirits in the heavenly sphere, evil spirits that are trying to manipulate and control the people we are praying for. When we acknowledge that it is not our loved ones but the Devil who is the true obstacle, our main prayer action should become clear. Our prayers should be focused on getting the Devil out of our loved ones' path.

As God's children, we have the privilege to exercise the authority that Jesus has given us to bind those evil spirits and keep them bound by means of prayer and Scriptures.

Scripture for Loved Ones

"For our struggle is not against flesh and blood, but against the rulers, against the authorities, against the powers of this dark world and against the spiritual forces of evil in the heavenly realms." (Ephesians 6:12 NIV)

"Therefore confess your sins to each other and pray for each other so that you may be healed. The prayer of a righteous person is powerful and effective." (James 5:16 NIV)

"Be completely humble and gentle; be patient, bearing with one another in love." (Ephesians 4:2 NIV)

"And let us consider how we may spur one another on toward love and good deeds." (Hebrews 10:24 NIV)

"For this reason, since the day we heard about you, we have not stopped praying for you. We continually ask God to fill you with the knowledge of his will through all the wisdom and understanding that the Spirit gives." (Colossians 1:9-12 NIV)

"Carry each other's burdens, and in this way you will fulfill the law of Christ." (Galatians 6:2 NIV)

"How wonderful and pleasant it is when brothers live together in harmony." (Psalm 133 NLT)

Prayers for Loved Ones

Show Them How to Take Control of Their Minds

Father God, I pray that You will show my loved ones how to take control of their minds and thoughts. I believe You search every heart and understand every motive behind our thoughts. I pray that they will accept You and serve You with wholehearted devotion and willing minds. I have confidence when they seek You they will find You. I pray they will seek You with all their minds, and that the words from their mouths, and the meditation of their hearts will be pleasing in Your sight.

Lord Jesus, I am thankful that all authority in heaven and on earth has been given to Your followers. In Your name, I take that authority today. I cast down and demolish every argument and everything that sets itself against the knowledge of You. I command all ungodly thoughts and desires that control my loved ones' minds to release them, never to return again. I command every proud obstacle that keeps them from knowing God, to be removed. I declare they are redeemed from their past, and they will find freedom, peace, and healing within their thoughts.

Holy Spirit, I pray my loved ones will remember that God is their rock and their redeemer. I pray they will keep in mind what God has redeemed them from. I pray You will take captive their every thought and make them obedient to Christ. Destroy every self-righteous barrier that keeps them from trusting Jesus as their Savior. I pray You will capture their defiant thoughts and persuade them to follow Christ. I declare that they are God's handiwork, created in Christ Jesus to do the good work that was prepared in advance for them.

In the precious name of Jesus I pray. Amen.

"We destroy every proud obstacle that keeps people from knowing God. We capture their rebellious thoughts and teach them to obey Christ." (2 Corinthians 10:5 NLT)

The Blood Covenant

Heavenly Father, I have faith that Jesus presides as the High Priest and He comes before Your throne as an advocate to mediate on my loved ones' behalf. I am certain that Christ's death and resurrection makes it possible for them to draw near to You. Through Jesus' bloodshed, they are rooted in a blood covenant, and they can enter into an intimate relationship with You and experience victory.

Father God, Thank You for the blood covenant that keeps us safe. I am confident because of the blood of Jesus we can boldly enter heaven's holy place. I apply the blood of Jesus over my loved ones hearts. I have faith that because of the blood of Jesus, they can confidently come to You. I have the full assurance of faith that You call us to persevere while we are here on earth so that we can go before Your throne boldly, entering into heaven in worship and prayer.

Father God, I am certain that Jesus' blood is the new covenant, which was shed for many for the remission of our sins. I am confident that my loved ones have been washed with clean water and sprinkled with the blood of Jesus and they are free from guilty consciences. I pray they will recognize that freedom and they will pursue a personal relationship with You.

Holy Spirit, I believe that You came to earth to be our comfort and strength. I pray You will comfort, strengthen, cover, and embrace my loved ones. I pray You will reach into their hearts and remove the things of this world that causes them discomfort and saturate them with God's unconditional love and grace.

In the precious name of Jesus I pray. Amen.

"And so, dear brothers and sisters, we can boldly enter heaven's Most Holy Place because of the blood of Jesus." (Hebrews 10:19 NLT)

Released and Set Free

Father God, as a disciple of Jesus Christ, I accept my God-given spiritual authority to exercise power over unclean spirits of all kinds. In the name of Your one and only Son, Jesus Christ, my Lord and Savior, I command every demonic invisible line that has been drawn around my loved ones to be erased by the blood of Jesus. I declare that they are released and free because they have not received a spirit of slavery that leads them to fear but a spirit of adoption as sons and daughters by which they cry out to You, Abba Father.

Lord Jesus, in Your name, I command all spirits that are not the Holy Spirit to depart from my loved ones'. I reach into their hearts and remove the rock of depression. I declare that Your light of happiness is shining in. I remove the moss of anger. I speak peace, harmony, and calmness. I tear down the dam of un-forgiveness. I build a bridge of forgiveness. I am certain that You are that bridge.

Lord Jesus, I cut the root of weakness and plant a vine of strength. I pull out the thorns of bad memories. I speak a future of victory. I rake leaves of rage, and water flowers of self-control. I sweep the dirt of hatred, and sow seeds of love and compassion. I weed the curse of failure, and gather harvest success. I tear down strongholds, and raise the Cross of Calvary in my loved ones' lives.

Father God, I pray that my loved ones will quickly come to accept that You are their loving Heavenly Father. I am certain with You all things are possible. I pray they will release all their fears and failures into Your capable hands. I declare that whatsoever I bind on earth shall be bound in heaven and whatsoever I released on earth shall be released in heaven.

In the precious name of Jesus I pray. Amen.

"For you have not received a spirit of slavery leading to fear again, but you have received a spirit of adoption as sons by which we cry out, 'Abba! Father." (Romans 8:15 NASB)

Parents' Salvation

Father God, thank You for the grace that restores and the grace that redeems. I believe that we are saved through that grace and the undeserved favor and mercy of Jesus. Help my parents see it is by grace through faith in Jesus that they are saved and salvation is a gift from You, not gained by their own works. I believe without a doubt that the Lord Jesus will save them the same way that He saves me through His mercy.

Heavenly Father, I am confident because I believe in the Lord Jesus Christ, my parents will also be saved. I am certain You will send a messenger by which my whole family shall be saved. I pray my parents will seek out an intimate relationship with You. I declare that they have deliverance, victory, peace, wholeness, and healing over all areas of their lives.

Holy Spirit, thank You for the protection You have set around my parents. I pray You will help them see that the kingdom of God is near and encourage them to repent and believe the good news. I pray You will take captive their every thought to make them obedient to Christ. Cast down and demolish every argument and every counterfeit thing that sets itself against the knowledge of God. I declare they are God's handiwork, created in Christ Jesus to do the good work that was prepared in advance for them.

Heavenly Father, I have confidence that when I ask, I shall receive, when I seek, I shall find, and when I knock, the door will be opened. I ask for You to open my parents' eyes to recognize Your saving grace. I seek the wisdom to truly honor and obey them. I realize that honoring my parents pleases You. I knock on the door of their hearts, and I pray that You will open their hearts. I pray You will give me the courage and the words to minister Your good news to them.

Father God, I trust in Your Word and hold tight to Your promise that You know the beginning from the end. I have faith that my parents will come to know Jesus as their Lord and Savior. I believe You rescued me so that the people I love could have Jesus within their reach. I desire to reflect the love and the light of Jesus to my parents. I want to do all that I can to assure that they will be in heaven with me.

In the precious name of Jesus I pray. Amen.

"We certainly believe that the Lord Jesus saves us the same way that he saves them through his kindness." (Acts 15:11 GW)

Long Life of Healing and Health for Parents

Lord Jesus, I am confident that You bore the stripes on Your back for all sin and iniquities and by those stripes, we are healed. I claim a supernatural healing of total health and well-being over my parents that can only come from You. I am certain the strength of those who wait with hope in You will be renewed. They will soar on wings like eagles. They will run and won't become weary. They will walk and won't grow tired.

Father God, thank You that our spiritual weapons are mighty and the authority of Jesus is far greater than the power of darkness, so the Enemy must yield. Therefore, in the name of Jesus Christ, I ask for a hedge of protection around my parents. I ask that Your warrior angels will preserve and protect them. I command all spirits of sickness to depart from my parents. I demand that the yoke of infections, pain, headaches, disease, virus, infirmities, and afflictions of any kind be destroyed. I cover them with the healing blood of Jesus.

Father God, I am convinced that You will satisfy my parents with a long life and You will show them their salvation. I pray for their physical, emotional, and spiritual healing. I have faith You are the healer of the brokenhearted and You are the one who bandages our wounds. I am confident that You will give them power when they are weak, When they have no might, You will increase their strength.

Heavenly Father, I am sure that You will rebuke the Devourer for my sake. I pray that You bind all strongholds from affecting my parents' as well as all curses that have been made against their ancestors.

I pray You will encourage my parents to wait upon You. Help them to understand that their faith in You assures them of the things they expect and convinces them of the things they cannot see.

Heavenly Father, I believe that You will answer my prayers and that anyone who is in trouble should call on You and You will rescue them. I have faith I do not need to worry about anything, but in every situation, I should let You know what I need in prayer while I give thanks. I declare You are my parents' healer, shield and refuge, their ever-present help in times of trouble. I have faith before they call, You will answer. While they are still speaking, You hear and come to their rescue.

In the precious name of Jesus I pray, Amen.

"I will satisfy you with a long life. I will show you how I will save you." (Psalm 91:16 GW)

Friends' Salvation

Father God, I pray You will help my friends' to see that the kingdom of God is near and encourage them to repent and believe the good news. Help them to comprehend it is by grace through faith in Jesus that they are saved, not the result of anything they can do, so they can not brag about it.

Holy Spirit, I pray that You will help my friends' understand and apply faith to their lives. I am convinced without faith, we can do nothing, for that reason we are all called to learn and develop our faith. I am certain that faith is essential and of the utmost importance for every aspect of our Christian life. I realize that faith comes from hearing the message about Christ. I pray You will give me the courage and the words to spread the message that Christ spoke.

Father God, I am convinced You rescued me so that the people I love could have Jesus within their reach. I pray I will reflect the love and the light of Jesus to my friends'. I want to do all that I can to help them spend eternity in heaven. I pray You will open the narrow door to their hearts and they will let Jesus come in. I pray You will give me opportunities to share my faith in Jesus to them.

Heavenly Father, I pray You will discourage and destroy every argument and every imaginary thing that sets itself against the knowledge of You. I pray You will take captive my friends' every thought to make them submissive to Christ. I declare that my friends will have salvation, victory, peace, wholeness, and healing. I have faith that You know the beginning from the end and that eternity with You will be their end.

In the precious name of Jesus I pray. Amen.

"So faith comes from hearing the message, and the message that is heard is what Christ spoke." (Romans 10:17 GW)

Spending Eternity in Heaven

Father God, I am convinced that no one is able to come to Jesus unless You attract and draw them and give them the desire to come. I pray that You will draw my loved one and they will have the desire to move towards Jesus, and they will follow Jesus all of their days. I have faith You will direct their steps and guide them in the right direction. I pray they will acquire spiritual understanding and walk in ways that is pleasing to You.

Father God, I am confident You desire for all to come to know Jesus as their Lord and Savior. You have opened Your kingdom to all who want to enter. I am certain Jesus is throwing open the doors to heaven, inviting us all in. I pray my loved ones' will understand that this life is just part of their journey home. That it is part of the process we take from this dark world to our real home You have waiting for us in heaven.

Heavenly Father, I pray that You will teach my loved ones to understand who You are and they will fully comprehend Your forgiveness. I pray You will open their hearts and shine Your light inside their spirits. Give them discernment so that they will move towards the truth. I pray without delay they will receive Jesus as their Lord and Savior and they will never slide away from Him. I pray You will pour out Your spirit upon them and they will receive the baptism of the Holy Spirit.

Holy Spirit, encourage my loved ones to have the unction to want to spend eternity in heaven. Reveal to them that Jesus is the way, the truth, and the life, and no one comes to the Father except through Him. I pray they will have the faith to confess with their mouths that Jesus is the Lord of all and believe in their hearts that God raised Him from the dead. I pray that nothing will stop them from spending eternity in heaven.

In the precious name of Jesus I pray. Amen.

"People cannot come to me unless the Father who sent me brings them to me. I will bring these people back to life on the last day." (John 6:44 GW)

Experience God's Presence through Repentance

Father God, I pray my loved ones will truly experience Your presence through repentance of their sins and they will be filled with a spirit of honesty, integrity, and sincerity. I pray the words on their lips and the actions that they take are pleasing in Your sight. I pray they will demonstrate true repentance and they will have hearts that are quick to confess their sins. Help them to truly regret their transgressions and turn away from them. I am confident You are faithful to cleanse and forgive their sins.

Holy Spirit, help my loved ones steer clear of making the same mistakes over and over again. Give them the strength and courage to turn away from any sinful ways. Cleanse them of their mistakes and iniquities. Create pure hearts in them and renew in them steadfast spirits. Fill them with a spirit of hope, love, joy, peace, and self-control.

Father God, I am so grateful that blessed are those whose transgressions are forgiven, whose sins are covered. I pray You will bring to my loved ones' attention every sin they are holding on to and encourage them to confess those sins so they can be forgiven. I pray that they will not live in condemnation. Help them see that the Holy Spirit convicts and the Devil condemns and help them to discern the difference between these two. I pray that they will truly see that You are faithful and just to forgive them when they confess and turn from their sins.

Heavenly Father, I declare I will live a life that reflects true repentance so that my loved ones can see Jesus living in me. I want to do all that I can to help everyone I love spend eternity with You. I believe that You rescued me so that the people I love could have Jesus within their reach. I pray they will feel You walking beside them. They will really look into Your eyes and see all the glory of Your power shining through. Help them to realize You have been with them all along. I pray they will feel something stirring inside their hearts and they will sense their emptiness fading away.

In the precious name of Jesus I pray. Amen.

"Create in me a pure heart, O God, and renew a steadfast spirit within me." (Psalm 51:10 NIV)

Family Salvation

Dear Heavenly Father, I am convinced that it is Your will for every individual to be saved, so I cry out to You for the salvation of my family. I pray You will shine Your light into their darkness.

Please do not wait another minute to call their names. I am certain that You will never leave their sides or turn Your back on them.

Father God, I pray my family will understand that it is with our hearts that we believe and are justified and with our mouths that we confess and are saved. I pray they will trust Jesus as their Savior by confessing with their mouths that Jesus is their Lord and they will receive Jesus as their Lord by believing in their hearts that You raised Him from the dead. I pray they will resolve to put You first in everything that they do and that they will never slide away from You.

Father God, I have faith In Your promise that when I trust in the Lord Jesus Christ, I am saved and my entire family will also be saved. I believe You will send a messenger through which my whole family will receive salvation. I am so grateful that I can see the good works You have already started in them. I trust You will carry them through to their completion, equipping them with everything they need to become spiritually mature in You.

Holy Spirit, I pray You will release God's angels to encamp around my family and a hedge of protection will surround them that will never be let down. I pray You will always encourage them to do what is right in God's eyes. I pray You will reveal to them God's faithfulness, kindness, patience, grace, and unfailing love.

Lord Jesus, when my family is off course and deceived place Your hand of deliverance upon them. I pray that they will understand that all men are born sinners and that no one will get into heaven by trying to be good enough. I pray that they will comprehend that it is only by having faith in You and You alone that will provide them their eternal salvation.

In the precious name of Jesus I pray. Amen.

"If you confess with your mouth that Jesus is Lord and believe in your heart that God raised him from the dead, you will be saved. For it is by believing in your heart that you are made right with God, and it is by confessing with your mouth that you are saved." (Romans 10:9-10 NLT)

Putting on the Full Armor of God

Lord Jesus, I pray that my loved ones will take up their shield of faith, with which they can extinguish all the flaming arrows of the Devil. I pray they will put on the helmet of salvation, and hold tight to the sword of the spirit, which is the Word of God. I pray they will stand firm with the belt of truth buckled around their waists. I pray they will put the breastplate of righteousness in place and they will slip their feet in to the readiness of the gospel of peace.

Father God, I pray my loved ones will obey authority when it lines up with Your Word and they will set their minds on heavenly thing. I pray they will always obey Your commands and their actions and choices are pleasing in Your sight. Teach them to have self-control, wearing faith and love as a breastplate and the hope of salvation as a helmet. Strengthen them so that they will not conform to the patterns of this world. Encourage them to become transformed by the renewing of their minds. I pray they will transform their attitudes and the thoughts of their minds for Your glory.

Heavenly Father, I pray each day my loved ones will be spiritually dressed for success so that they can stand firm in the battles of life. I pray that each morning they will put every piece of the armor of God on. That they will dress themselves in truth, righteousness, peace, faith, salvation, the Word, and they will pray without ceasing. Help them to see that these are absolutely essential to every believer and without them; we cannot go into any battle and come out of it victorious.

Lord Jesus, I declare our spiritual weapons are mighty and the authority You have given us is far greater than the power of darkness, so the Enemy must admit defeat. I have faith with the whole armor of God we are able to stand against whatever the Devil attempts. In Your name, I take my God-given authority. I command that all behaviors that are ungodly or destructive come to an end in my loved ones' lives. I command that all spirits that are not the Holy Spirit must depart from them. I order all strongholds and all generational curses placed against them, to be removed this very moment.

In the precious name of Jesus I pray. Amen.

The Whole Armor of God: (Ephesians 6:13-17 ESV)

Renewing Health and Restoration

Father God, I am confident You are the healer of the brokenhearted. You are the one who bandages our wounds. I have faith You forgive all our sins and heal all our diseases. I proclaim that Jesus bore the stripes on His back for all sin and iniquities and by those stripes, my loved ones are healed and restored. I proclaim the precious blood of Jesus over them. I claim a supernatural healing that only comes from You. I declare the yoke of sickness, pain, and disease is destroyed.

Holy Spirit, teach my loved ones to wait upon the Lord so they can renew their strength, and they run, and not be weary, and walk, and not be faint. I have confidence You are their shield and refuge, their ever-present help in times of trouble. I am certain You give them power when they are weak. When they have no might, You restore their strength.

Father God, I declare our spiritual weapons are mighty and the authority of Jesus is far greater than the power of darkness, so the Enemy must surrender. I believe You will rebuke the Devourer and bring to an end all strongholds and all curses that have been made against my loved ones' and You will keep them from affecting their health and well-being. I pray they will experience renewed health and restoration.

In the precious name of Jesus I pray. Amen.

"He forgives all my sins and heals all my diseases." (Psalm 103:3 NLT)

Maintaining Good Family Relationships

Father God, I pray for healing and restoration over my family relationships. I pray You will purge any un-forgiveness they are holding on to and continually remind them of Your forgiveness toward them. Remove from my family any unresolved feelings and replace those feelings with Your peace, which surpasses all understanding. I pray You will saturate their hearts with love and compassion toward each other. I have faith that You will shape them into the creation that You have fashioned them to be before the foundation of this world.

Father God, I pray my family will respect, appreciate, and admire each other. Give them the desire to want to know their family better. Encourage them to make the time to get to know each other. I pray for a close, happy, peaceful, and uncomplicated relationship with family members. Help them to accept each other for who they are.

Holy Spirit, I pray You will persuade my family to resolve any quarrels or misunderstandings. Teach them to be the first to say that they are sorry and the first to say that they forgive. Then help them to put the incidents behind them and move forward. I pray they will have the compassion to forgive, as You command us to do.

Father God, I pray You will bring reconciliation to my family so that we will wake up to our common Enemy. Give us the wisdom to do whatever we need to do to remove the walls, and fight together to drive out any wedge that Satan has tried to place between family members. I pray that this reconciliation will bring healing and restoration to those relationships.

Father God, I pray You will place hearts for forgiveness in my family members. Take away all their pride and humble their hearts. Fill them with the love of Jesus and mold them into His image. I pray they will be of one mind with compassion towards one another and that their relationships today, tomorrow, and forever will please You.

In the precious name of Jesus I pray. Amen.

"Then fill me with joy by having the same attitude and the same love, living in harmony, and keeping one purpose in mind." (Philippians 2:2 GW)

Creating a Joyful Home

Father God, it is my desire to create a joyful home. Therefore I have made the decision to speak only words of encouragement in my home so that my family's walk of faith will mature. I will also give them the support, respect, kindness, and help they need and deserve. I declare I will not irritate or provoke my family to anger, but I will encourage them joyfully, tenderly, and faithfully in godly training, discipline, and counsel. I am confident I honor You by being faithful to them.

Holy Spirit, encourage me to only speak what is good for edifying so that my words minister grace and joy to my family. I declare that I will not allow corrupt communication to proceed out of my mouth toward them. I declare I am sensitive to the anointing that God has placed on them. I will encourage them to increase in their walks of faith. I pray my joyful attitude in my home will inspire happiness. I pray my family will celebrate in God's presence, overflowing with joy.

Heavenly Father, I am certain that our home is redeemed from the curse of destruction, sickness, poverty, debt, and death, because You rebuke the Devourer for our namesake. I bind the hands of the Enemy in any way that he comes to kill, steal, or destroy our joyful home. I discharge Your warrior angels to go forth now to guard and protect our home.

In the precious name of Jesus I pray. Amen.

"But let righteous people rejoice. Let them celebrate in God's presence. Let them overflow with joy." (Psalm 68:3 GW)

Increasing in Faith

Heavenly Father, I am confident we all have been given a measure of faith and all we need is faith the size of a mustard seed to move mountains. I pray the faith that You have given my loved ones will become mountain-moving faith. I pray You will increase their faith. Reveal to them that faith in You gives them the confidence that what they hope for will actually happen and the assurance about the things they cannot see.

Holy Spirit, I am certain that salvation is an act of faith in our Lord Jesus Christ. I believe we are all called to develop faith because faith is essential and of the utmost importance for every aspect of our Christian walk. I pray You will help my loved ones to see that without faith, we can do nothing. I pray You will teach them how to develop and apply their faith.

Father God, I pray my loved ones will understand because of faith, our spiritual weapons are mighty and the authority of Jesus is far greater than the power of darkness, so the Enemy must yield. I pray that they will realize that faith has set them free, and with faith in Jesus they have the authority to rebuke the Devourer, and bind Satan's strongholds, and curses from affecting their lives.

In the precious name of Jesus I pray. Amen.

"Faith is the confidence that what we hope for will actually happen; it gives us assurance about things we cannot see." (Hebrews 11:1 NLT)

A Life Devoted to Jesus

Father God, I pray that my loved ones will fix their eyes on Jesus, the author and finisher of their faith. I pray they will live a life devoted to Jesus and they will come to love You with their whole mind, heart, and soul. I pray they will appreciate what Jesus has done for them and they will totally surrender to Him.

Holy Spirit, I pray my loved ones will confess with their mouths that Jesus is their Lord and believe in their hearts that God has raised Him from the dead so that they will be saved. I pray they will confess that they have been crucified with Christ and that they no longer live but that it is Christ who lives within them. Open their eyes to see that God so loved the world that He gave His only begotten Son and whoever believes in Jesus should not perish but will have everlasting life. I pray they will believe and receive everlasting life in the fullest. Help them to see when we believe in Jesus, we don't just receive the forgiveness of sins but we are raised up with Jesus to share in His place of honor.

Father God, I pray my loved ones will truly be devoted followers of the Lord, making the time to sit at the feet of Jesus, listening to what He has to say. I pray they will totally commit themselves to Jesus. I pray their devotion to the Lord will come from hearts of love, faithfulness, and loyalty. I pray they will see the world through Jesus' eyes, and they will become more like Him.

Holy Spirit, encourage my loved ones to read the Bible daily and do what it proclaims. Give them revelations so they can cast off restraints. I pray they will understand that God's Word is a lamp to their feet and a light to their path. Reveal to them that when they read the Bible regularly, they will come to know God intimately, and gain strength and wisdom.

In the precious name of Jesus I pray. Amen.

"Is not my word like as a fire? saith the Lord; and like a hammer that breaketh the rock in pieces?" (Jeremiah 23:29 KJV)

Standing Firm in the Faith

Lord Jesus, I pray my loved ones will put on the full armor of God so that they can take their stand against the Devil's schemes. Encourage them to be on their guard, to stand firm in the faith, to be courageous and strong. Help them to understand it is for freedom that You have set us free. I pray they will understand that through faith and God's grace, they can boast in the hope and the glory of God.

Father God, I am certain that a man's heart plans his way but You direct his steps. I pray my loved one will stand their ground in their walks with You and You will guide them down the paths that You have planned for them. I pray they will grow in the grace and knowledge of the Lord and Savior, Jesus Christ.

Father God, I pray my loved ones will stand firm, so that they will win in life. Help them to see their labor in the Lord is not in vain so that they will stand firm. I pray that nothing will move them and they will always give themselves fully to the work of the Lord. I pray they will understand by standing firm in their faith, You bless them in the heavenly realms with every spiritual blessing in Christ.

Holy Spirit, I pray You will teach my loved ones Your ways and lead them down narrow roads. Help them to stand firm and not be burdened down by the yoke of slavery. Rather, let them clothe themselves with the Lord Jesus Christ. I have confidence when trials begin to take place, You will give them the strength and courage to stand up and lift up their heads because their redemption is drawing near.

In the precious name of Jesus I pray. Amen.

"For this reason, take up all the armor that God supplies. Then you will be able to take a stand during these evil days. Once you have overcome all obstacles, you will be able to stand your ground." (Ephesians 6:13 GW)

Overcoming Addictions and Strongholds

Heavenly Father, I cry out to You on the behalf of my loved ones. I pray that they will allow You to take control of their lives. I pray that You will shelter them from all addictions and strongholds. Deliver them from any unhealthy addictions particularly (name strongholds). Help them to see that their bodies are not their own but their bodies are the Holy Spirit's temples. Persuade them when they are engaged in anything that is harmful to their health or relationships.

Holy Spirit, warn my loved ones that harmful living will cause them to slowly fall into death. Reveal to them that Jesus came to deliver them. Explain to them that God promises not only to look out for them as they go into the battle but also to be their rear guard after the battle. Reveal to them that the weapons they fight with are not the weapons of this world but ones of divine power to tear down strongholds. Remind them that they have the authority to demolish every argument and every pretense that sets itself up against the knowledge of God. Reveal to them that they have the authority to take captive every thought to make it obedient to Christ.

Father God, I pray my loved ones will totally surrender their hearts to Jesus and receive His great healing power and feel His comfort in their pain. I pray they will be set free from evil and will lay their pasts at the feet of Jesus. I pray they will gain the strength to say yes to the things that bring life and they will find the courage to eliminate anything from their personality that would bring them toward these harmful behaviors. I pray You will impart to them the discernment and the will to turn away from anything that leads to death, disease, and heartbreak.

Heavenly Father, rebuke the Devourer and prevent the Devil from destroying my loved ones' lives with devastating habits. I declare that no weapon formed against them shall prosper. I pray You will open their eyes to see the truth in every situation. I pray You will become their only dependence.

Lord Jesus, in Your name, I declare that my loved ones are rescued, healed, and saved. I speak to all ancestral curses that have been passed down. I demand them to release my loved ones. I declare that they are unshackled and set free. They belong to You and they are under the blood that You shed for them. Help them to see that You are their Savior and rescuer.

In the precious name of Jesus I pray. Amen.

"The weapons we use in our fight are not made by humans. Rather, they are powerful weapons from God. With them we destroy people's defenses, that is, their arguments and all their intellectual arrogance that oppose the knowledge of God. We take every thought captive so that it is obedient to Christ." (2 Corinthians 10:4-5 GW)

Freedom from Rebellious Behavior

Father God, I pray that my loved ones will desire to obey You as their heavenly Father. I have faith that You can change their hearts, minds, and actions. I pray they will be uncomfortable with sin, evil, and worldly things. Give them sweet and humble hearts so that they will walk in obedience with You.

Holy Spirit, I pray that my loved ones will work cheerfully as if they are serving their heavenly Father and not merely serving people. I am convinced that our Heavenly Father rewards all of us for the good we do. I pray they will achieve freedom from rebellious behavior. Strengthen them to work wholeheartedly at everything and help them to recognize that they are serving God with their outstanding performance.

Father God, encourage my loved ones to respect and to be obedient toward You and toward authority so that their lives will be long and excellent. I am confident that You know their disobedience and their every thought. I pray they will not give themselves over to pride and selfishness. I pray that all the rebellion they are displaying will come to an end today.

Heavenly Father, I take my God-given authority in the name of Jesus. I stand against the schemes of the Devil. I demand idolatry, rebellion, stubbornness, and disrespect to leave my loved ones this moment. I declare that rebellious behavior will have no part in their lives. I proclaim that Jesus gave us the gift of life, abundant life, and the new life Christ provides for us is complete and lacking in nothing.

Father God, I have faith that Jesus can take away, their pain, anger, rebellion, and chaos. I declare that my loved ones will not walk in the path of death or destruction. I declare that Jesus has set them free from rebellious behavior and whoever the Lord has set free is free indeed.

In the precious name of Jesus I pray. Amen.

"Serve eagerly as if you were serving your heavenly master and not merely serving human masters. You know that your heavenly master will reward all of us for whatever good we do, whether we're slaves or free people." (Ephesians 6:7-8 GW)

Deliverance from Substance Abuse

Heavenly Father, I pray that You will deliver my loved ones from all addictions, particularly cigarettes, alcohol, and drugs of any kind. Bring to an end any plans that the Devil may have to destroy or addict them. Remove from them anything within them that would lead them to this destructive behavior. I pray that they will have discernment to say no to the things that lead to death and say yes to things that lead to life.

Father God, I pray my loved ones will fix their eyes on Jesus and allow Him to take control over their entire lives. Show them they do not belong to themselves and help them to realize that their bodies are a temple of the Holy Spirit. I pray You will nudge them to stop if they try anything that is harmful to their well-being. I pray their only addiction is Jesus and that they use their bodies to give You glory.

Holy Spirit, I pray my loved ones will run the race that lies ahead of them and they will never give up. I pray they will get rid of everything that slows them down, especially the sin that distracts them. Help them to discern and break free from what is slowly destroying the beautiful things in their lives like their marriages, families, friendships, ministries, health, and their walks with God. Give them the courage and strength to throw off the misbehaviors that so easily entangle them and everything that hinders them from running the race God has marked out for them.

Father God, I pray You will enable me to minister to my loved ones with kindness and understanding. I am confident that the Holy Spirit is with me and has equipped me to speak the truth to them. I believe You have sent me to declare forgiveness to those enslaved in sin and to help the blind to see the light of Jesus. I pray the Holy Spirit will speak through me so I can share Your grace and mercy with those who have been shattered by sin. I pray that Your anointing will come upon me so I can accomplish these things.

Father God, in the name of Jesus, I command that all spirits that are not the Holy Spirit depart from my loved ones. I break all ancestral curses from either side of their families. I demand that Satan release my loved ones from all addictions that control them. I pray they will choose life and truth in every decision they make. I proclaim that my loved ones are under the blood covenant of Jesus.

In the precious name of Jesus I pray. Amen.

"The Spirit of the Lord is upon Me, because He has anointed Me to preach the gospel to the poor; He has sent Me to heal the brokenhearted, to proclaim liberty to the captives and recovery of sight to the blind, to set at liberty those who are oppressed." (Luke 4:18 NKJV)

Gaining a Sense of Self-Worth

Father God, I pray that my loved ones will feel loved and accepted first by You and then by others. Give them high self-esteem yet teach them to be humble. I pray You will bathe their hearts with Your never-ending love and they will realize that You love them so much that You sent Your one and only Son to die for them.

Holy Spirit, help my loved ones see that Jesus thought they were so precious that He poured out His life for every wrong thing they have ever done—or will ever do. Encourage them to see that their inner selves, their unfading beauty, and their gentle and quiet spirits are of great worth in God's sight. I pray You will make clear to them that all their talents, experiences, struggles, weaknesses, and strengths are all a divine tapestry to make them everything they need to be to accomplish all that God put them here to do.

Heavenly Father, I pray that You will illustrate Your loving kindness in the morning and Your soft whisper in the evening. I pray my loved ones will feel Your endless love penetrate their hearts, minds and spirits. I am confident if they trust in You at all times and abide in the love of Jesus, they are blessed with the awesome gift of love that You give freely.

Father God, I pray that You will deliver my loved ones from all the lies that the Devil has spoken against them. I pray that You will release all doubt and unworthiness from their minds. Help them to identify that You gave them their worth and their real worth comes from being close to You. In the name of Jesus, I demand all curses that have been spoken against them and all words that would diminish their senses of self-worth to release my loved ones this very moment.

In the precious name of Jesus I pray. Amen.

"Rather, beauty is something internal that can't be destroyed. Beauty expresses itself in a gentle and quiet attitude which God considers precious." (1 Peter 3:4 GW)

Pleading the Blood of Jesus for Deliverance, Protection, and Forgiveness

Father God, I pray that You will draw near with Your supernatural power to bring freedom, healing, and deliverance to my loved ones particular situations. I pray for their physical, emotional, and mental healing. I pray for their recovery from prescription and illegal drugs, cigarette, and alcohol addictions. I pray for victory over demons, evil people, and for any kind of battle that will come their way. I am certain only You know when attacks will come and only You can protect and shield them from these attacks before they appear. I pray You will move in with Your full divine protection before any of these assaults can approach my loved ones.

Heavenly Father, I am certain that pleading the blood of Jesus is the greatest, aggressive, spiritual weapons that I have in my spiritual arsenal. I have faith when I plead the blood of Jesus on my loved ones specific circumstances they will have freedom and victory in those areas. I have full confidence when Jesus shed His blood at Calvary the new covenant began. His blood was shed for all, for deliverance, protection, and forgiveness of our sins.

Lord Jesus, thank You for the authority to trample on serpents and scorpions, for the power to destroy the enemy, and for the promise that nothing shall by any means hurt us. I take that powerful authority and I plead Your shed blood over every inch of my loved ones bodies, souls, and spirits, over their families, homes, finances, offices, work places, over their spouses, and their children, over their cars, and any transportation they may ride in.

Father God, in the name of Jesus, I plead the blood of Jesus against any demons that is trying to come against my loved ones. I plead the blood of Jesus against any bad and evil people who are trying to harm them. In the name of Jesus, I plead the blood of Jesus against any natural accidents or catastrophes that may come close to them. I plead the blood of Jesus against any diseases, viruses, or illnesses that could possibly attack them.

Gracious Father, in the name of Jesus, I have full faith and certainty that the blood of Jesus will fully protect my loved ones against all of the things that I have just pleaded His blood over. I am certain it is not by might, nor by power, but by Your Spirit, that we receive forgiveness, deliverance, and protection.

In the precious name of Jesus I pray. Amen.

"I have given you the authority to trample snakes and scorpions and to destroy the enemy's power. Nothing will hurt you." Luke 10:19 (GW)

CHAPTER 5

Praying for Finances

Blessings for Obedience!

To gain victory in our finances, we need to abide by the principles in God's Word. If you are experiencing problems in the area of your finances, examine God's Word to find out what He teaches in regard to finances and come into agreement with Him. Ask yourself, "Am I truly being a good steward with what God has entrusted to me by handling money wisely?" Keep in mind that it's God who gives us the power to gain wealth.

Being totally committed to God is the very first step toward financial blessing. As Christians, we are promised blessings and prosperity from God, not the curse of poverty. Christ redeemed us from the curse of the law by becoming a curse for us. He redeemed us so that the blessing given to Abraham found in Deuteronomy 28 might come to us through Him. When we obey the Lord and faithfully follow all His commands, then all the blessings described in Deuteronomy 28 will come to us. We have the promise that the Lord will open the heavens of His rich storehouse. He will send miracles at the right time and bless everything we do.

No matter what we are experiencing, we should be fully committed and thankful to God. As Christians, we have no need to be anxious about anything but we should bring everything to God by means of prayer and petition with thanksgiving. We should be seeking God and His will by entrusting all our money and material things to Him and trusting Him to bring about our prosperity.

Give freely with your finances!

True financial wisdom comes from God, and the Bible has instructions about how we should handle our finances. I believe we will find financial freedom when we agree with the Word of God in this matter. God commands us to bring the whole tithe (10 percent) into His storehouse. This means that we are to give at least 10 percent to His kingdom and that we should give our tithe to the church we attend. We are instructed to honor the Lord with our wealth and our "first fruits." That means we tithe before we pay other bills.

We are instructed to give freely to the poor and always to be generous in giving to others, not withholding good from those who deserve it. The Bible warns us that if we close our eyes to the poor, we will receive many curses. Remember, God loves a cheerful giver, and when we sow in the kingdom of God, we can be certain that with the measure we use, it will be measured back unto us.

Be accountable with your finances!

It is important to not go into debt over foolish things. We need to do our best not to be wasteful with our money. Jesus warns us about gathering treasures on earth because treasures on earth can break, get stolen, deteriorate, or be damaged. Instead Jesus encourages us to store up treasures in heaven where they will last forever. Some ways we can store up treasures in heaven are by financially helping others, giving money to Gods kingdom, sharing Jesus with our friends and family, spending time at church worshipping, learning, and volunteering.

Think about where your treasure is, because there, your heart will also be. Ask yourself, "Are the things I buy wasteful?" God warns us that those who love pleasure will become poor, so we should not seek for our own benefit but the benefit of others. We should not become selfish, spending our finances on our own self-centered desires. Keep in mind we cannot take anything out of this world.

Trusting the Lord with your Finances!

We must have faith that our help comes from the Lord and trust that He is our provider. God told us He would bless the works of our hands. That's why, we should think of work as a reward from God, and we should not be lazy or uncaring at our jobs. Our work ethic is very important to God because it demonstrates our Christian character to others. Therefore, we should make every effort to do our jobs with all our might, as if we are working for the Lord, and we should have faith He will promote us in His timing.

Paying your Debts!

In addition, past due debt needs to be addressed. We are instructed to let no debt remain outstanding, so we should pay all outstanding debts or make arrangements to do so, even when we are experiencing financial difficulties, because this is pleasing to God. God will honor our effort to do what we have promised.

Forgiving others!

There may also be areas in our life such as un-forgiveness that could be stopping financial blessing. We are commanded to forgive others when they sin against us. Ask the Holy Spirit to reveal any un-forgiveness or bitterness that is hindering your financial blessings and then release those people of their transgressions against you.

Scriptures for Finances

"Remember the Lord your God. He is the one who gives you power to be successful, in order to fulfill the covenant he confirmed to your ancestors with an oath." (Deuteronomy 8:18 NLT)

"Therefore keep the words of this covenant and do them that you may prosper in all that you do." (Deuteronomy 29:9 ESV)

"Trust the Lord your God, and believe. Believe his prophets, and you will succeed." (2 Chronicles 20:20 GW)

By humility and the fear of the LORD are riches, and honor, and life." (Proverbs 22:4 KJV)

"'For I know the plans I have for you,' says the Lord. 'They are plans for good and not for disaster, to give you a future and a hope." (Jeremiah 29:11 NLT)

"The thief's purpose is to steal and kill and destroy. My purpose is to give them a rich and satisfying life." (John 10:10 NLT)

"Dear friend, I know that you are spiritually well. I pray that you're doing well in every other way and that you're healthy." (3 John 1:2 GW)

Prayers for Finances

The Whole Tithe Is Holy

Father God, I come into agreement with You. I choose to bring one-tenth of my income into Your storehouse, so that there may be food in Your house. I am certain by passing this test that You will open the windows of heaven on me and flood me with blessings, that there shall not be room enough for me to receive them. I have confidence when I am faithful with my tithes and offerings that You will shower down financial blessing over my life, my businesses, and my household.

Father God, thank You for pouring out blessings on me, for the financial miracles I have already received, and for the ones yet to come. I pray that You will continue to abundantly bless my household. It is my desire to live a debt-free life so that I can without restraint pour back into Your kingdom. I pray You will deliver me right now from all debt and give me the wisdom to never accumulate debt again.

Holy Spirit, give me godly wisdom so I can be a good steward over all that I have been entrusted with. I declare with the measure I am given, I will give to the church, the poor, the neglected, the mission field, and whomever You prompt me to. I stand in agreement with God's Word and proclaim everything I put my hands on shall prosper. I declare and claim ridiculous amounts of wealth.

In the precious name of Jesus I pray. Amen.

"'Bring one-tenth of your income into the storehouse so that there may be food in my house. Test me in this way,' says the Lord of Armies. 'See if I won't open the windows of heaven for you and flood you with blessings." (Malachi 3:10 GW)

Debts Paid in Full

Heavenly Father, I have confidence when I obey Your Word and walk in faith, all I need is faith the size of a mustard seed to move mountains. I am convinced You have blessed me in the heavenly realm with every spiritual blessing in Christ Jesus. Therefore by faith in Jesus and on the authority of Your Holy Word, I speak to my mountain of debt. Debt I speak to you in the name of Jesus and command you to be paid, be gone, vanish, and cease to exist. I declare and command all my debts, credit cards, loans, mortgages, and notes are paid in full, canceled, dissolved, or forgiven. I call all my debts paid in full.

Father God, I realize that nothing incredible can be accomplished by me. I have faith You will give me both the ability and the power to accomplish this by liberally supplying every need through Your riches in glory by Christ Jesus. It is my desire to owe no one anything; I only want to love others, because the one who loves another has fulfilled the law. I will make it my goal to live quietly, do my work and earn my own living, so that my way of life will win respect from others, and I will not have to depend on anyone else for what I need. I declare whatever I do; I will work heartily, for You and not for men. I choose to seek first Your kingdom and Your righteousness. I have faith all good things will be added to me.

In the precious name of Jesus I pray. Amen.

"And my God will liberally supply (fill to the full) your every need according to His riches in glory in Christ Jesus." (Philippians 4:19 AMP)

Increasing in Godly Prosperity

Father God, thank You for the assurance that despite any present difficulties that I may be experiencing, You still have plans for me, plans to increase me and restore me. I have faith that Your promises still remain true. I believe that You know my struggles and You are working to help me flourish, even when I can't see it. I am confident that You know the plans that You have for me, plans to prosper me and not to harm me, plans to give me a hope and a future.

Father God, I am confident when I pursue righteousness and love, I find life, prosperity, and honor. I am certain as Your child that riches, honor, enduring wealth, prosperity, and blessings belong to me. I pray that You will always allow the light of Your face to shine on me. I desire to always be connected to You like a tree planted near fresh water. I have faith that through obedience, I will prosper and thrive because I am permanently connected to the true source of life. I have faith when I submit to You, I will be at peace and prosperity will come to me.

Heavenly Father, I am certain that it is You who gives me the ability to produce wealth, and I will eat the fruit of my labor. Blessings and prosperity shall be abundant in my life. I am determined to do my best and walk in obedience. I have no doubt that if I obey and serve You, I will spend the rest of my days in prosperity and contentment and my descendants will inherit the land.

In the precious name of Jesus I pray. Amen.

"I know the plans that I have for you, declares the Lord. They are plans for peace and not disaster plans to give you a future filled with hope." (Jeremiah 29:11 GW)

Obtaining Financial Freedom

Heavenly Father, I declare I shall obtain financial freedom by becoming debt-free. I am certain if I hold on patiently for Your financial blessings, I will receive what I need for my financial breakthrough. I believe that whatever purpose You have in mind, it will be accomplished. I have faith that the end of a matter is better than the beginning. I realize that whether or not it looks like I am succeeding, You have a plan for my finances.

Father God, I have faith that what You have spoken goes out from Your mouth and will not return to You empty but will accomplish what You desire and achieve the purpose for which You sent it. I am grateful that Your thoughts are not my thoughts. Neither are my ways Your ways. I am convinced that Your ways are greater than my ways and Your thoughts are higher than my thoughts.

Lord Jesus, thank You for the authority that You have given me to speak directly to my mountains. I speak to my mountains of deficiency, incompleteness, inadequacy, poverty, hardship, adversity, insufficiency, debt, and shortage. I command them to depart from my life, my businesses, and my finances, never to return again.

Holy Spirit, I pray You will assist me in being a good steward of God's resources. It is my desire to take the blessings and prosperity that God has given to me and use them to bless others. I am certain the way that I give of my money, my possessions, and my time is evidence of my love for God. I declare I will put all my trust in Jehovah Jireh as I move toward a place of financial freedom because I am certain my Lord will provide.

Father God, I believe that I am a money manager for Your kingdom. I realize that You own it all and my job is to wisely take care of what You have entrusted to me. I am honored that You have chosen me to help finish the work Jesus came to do.

In the precious name of Jesus I pray. Amen.

"So shall my word be that goeth forth out of my mouth: it shall not return unto me void, but it shall accomplish that which I please, and it shall prosper in the thing whereto I sent it." (Isaiah 55:11 KJV)

Ask, Seek, and Knock for Financial Blessings

Father God, Your Word tells me to ask in order to receive. I ask and I have faith to receive business deals that close and produce large commissions. I ask and I have faith to receive wisdom and knowledge when I'm investing money and purchasing property and possessions. I ask and have faith to receive prosperity, wealth, success, riches, assets, resources, investments properties, homes, capital, funds, reserves, profit, and revenue. I ask and have faith to receive an increase in my earning of a thousand times more than I am right now. I ask and have faith to receive growth and multiplication in my investments and businesses. I ask and have faith to receive blessing and favor. I ask and have faith to receive that my gifts and talents will develop and mature.

Father God, Your Word tells me to seek in order to find. I seek and have faith I will find You and Your will for my life. I seek and have faith that I will find Your Word over my finances. I declare what You have spoken goes out from Your mouth and will not return to You empty but will accomplish what You desire and achieve the purpose for which You sent it. I seek and have faith I will find all that You have planned for me. I seek and have faith I will find the blessing and favor You have for me. I seek and have faith that I will find the positions You have ordained for me before the foundation of this world.

Father God, Your Word tells me that if I knock, the door will be opened. I knock and have faith the door will be opened for wisdom. I pray for the wisdom to make sound financial decisions and the wisdom to knock on the right doors. I knock and have faith the door will be opened to financial opportunities that will produce an abundant amount of income. I knock and have faith the door will be opened to business transactions and clients for financial increase. I knock and have faith the door will be opened for favor first with You and then with men. I knock and have faith the doors will be opened that You want me to walk through, that no man can shut.

In the precious name of Jesus I pray. Amen.

"And so I tell you, keep on asking, and you will receive what you ask for. Keep on seeking, and you will find. Keep on knocking, and the door will be opened to you." (Luke 11:9 NLT)

Receiving Financial Blessings

Heavenly Father, I am so grateful that You own the universe and I am Your child, an heir with Christ Jesus. I have faith that I am blessed and I will receive an inheritance as a reward because I place all my hope and trust in You. I declare You are my shepherd and I shall not want. I am confident when I entrust my plans to You, they shall succeed. I will work at everything I do with all my heart as if I am working for You.

Father God, I pray that You will make me financially successful. I declare by faith that You will meet all my needs according to the riches of Your glory in Christ Jesus. I pray that You will continue to bless me beyond measure with ridiculous amounts of money. I praise You for the financial blessings I have already received and the ones yet to come.

Father God, I desire that no debt I owe remain outstanding, except for the debt to continually love others. I pray for godly wisdom so that I can be a good steward over all that I have been entrusted with. It is my desire to do things Your way. I stand in agreement with Your Word and proclaim everything I put my hand on shall prosper.

Father God, I am certain that when I give to Your kingdom, blessings will be given back to me in good measure, pressed down, shaken together and running over into my lap. I pray that every seed I sow will be acceptable in Your sight and You will give me the wisdom to sow on fruitful ground. I declare with the blessings I am given, I will give to the church, the poor, to the mission field, to my loved ones, and to whomever else You tell me too.

Father God, I pray You will guide me in all my ways and direct my steps as I wait patiently for You. I trust that You will hear my prayers and turn to me and that I will receive financial victory. I believe You respond to the prayers of the needy and You know all of my needs, wants, and requests. I have faith that You will provide for all of my needs before I speak and that You will help me even while I am still asking.

In the precious name of Jesus I pray. Amen.

"But my God shall supply all your need according to his riches in glory by Christ Jesus." (Philippians 4:19 KJV)

Blessing for Obedience

Father God, I have faith in Your Word, and I hold tight to Your promises. I believe that if I obey You and carefully follow all the commands You have given me, You will set me on high above all the nations on earth, and Your blessings will come on me, and accompany me. I am confident You will bless me in the city and bless me in the country. I declare wherever I go, I will be blessed.

Father God, I pray that my children and all my possessions will be blessed. I have faith that my pantries and closets will always be full. I am blessed when I come in and blessed when I go out. I am blessed when I leave my home and blessed when I return home.

Holy Spirit, release my angels to surround me and protect me wherever I go. I have faith that all the enemies who rise up against me will be defeated before me. They may come at me from one direction, but they will flee from me in seven.

Father God, I believe that You will send a blessing on my workplace and on everything I put my hands on. I declare my checking accounts, savings accounts, investments, and my retirement funds will overflow. I am confident You have blessed the land that You have given me. I have faith that my home is blessed.

I have faith that You will establish me as one of Your holy people because You promised me that if I keep Your commands and walk in obedience with You. Then all the peoples on earth will see that I am called by the name of the Lord.

Father God, I have faith that You will grant me abundant prosperity and will lavish me with good things. I pray that You will open the heavens and the storehouse of Your bounty to send rain on my land in season and bless all the works of my hands. I declare that my businesses and endeavors are blessed. I have faith that I will lend too many but will borrow from none. I have confidence I am blessed so that I can be a blessing to others.

Father God, I pray You will help me to stay on the path You have planned for me. Help me to keep Your commands. Give me the ability to succeed in all that I do. I have faith that You will make me the head and not the tail. I declare that I will be a leader to my family, my church, my businesses, and my community because I pay attention to the commands that You have given me and I work to carefully follow them. I have faith I will always be at the top and never at the bottom. I declare I will not turn aside from any of the commandments that You have given me, either to the right or to the left. I will not follow other gods or serve them.

In the precious name of Jesus I pray. Amen.

Blessings from the Lord. (Deuteronomy 28:1-14 GW)

Blessed and Thankful

Father God, I am so grateful for the second chances that You have given me and for the pits that You have rescued me from. I am certain when I place all my trust in You; I am blessed beyond measure. I am thankful for Your unfailing grace and mercy. Thank You for all the blessings in disguise, through them You have been the source of my strength.

Father God, thank You for preserving and restoring my health and for providing for all of my needs. I am confident it is You who gives me everything I have ever needed or asked for. Thank You for all the little things and all the big things that You are doing right now to show me Your love.

Heavenly Father, it is my desire to be blessed so that I can bless others. I am so thankful for the blessings You shower down on my life. Over the years, I have seen You provide for all of my needs. You have blessed me in countless ways; I can't even begin to understand. I declare everything that You give me, I will give back to You. I desire to put everything You bless me with to good use for Your kingdom here on earth. I desire to be like a seed planted in good soil to embrace Your Word and produce good fruit—a harvest above my wildest dreams.

Father God, I ask for Your perfect will to be done in my life. I am tired of small things. I trust You to make my life so much bigger, bigger than I ever thought it could be for Your kingdom's cause and for Your glory.

In the precious name of Jesus I pray. Amen.

"O LORD of hosts, Blessed is the man who trusts in You." (Psalms 84:12 NKJV)

Authority over Finances

Heavenly Father, by the authority delegated to me in the name of Jesus Christ, I imprison Satan and render him powerless in my financial situation. As a matter of record, Satan you are forever imprisoned in the Name of Jesus. I cast out the spirits of mismanagement, poverty, lack, failure, bankruptcy, decline, debt. I release into each category just mentioned wisdom, resourcefulness, influence, profit, increase, creativity, truth, honesty, revenue, and prosperity.

Father God, I take authority as Your child and call my debts paid. I speak to my finances and tell them to come in line with Your Word. I believe that I am blessed with the promise of Abraham because I observe Your commandments. I declare I am the head and not the tail. I am above and not beneath. I declare that You are my source and that recession, inflation, and every other economic breakdown doesn't belong to me. I am more than a conqueror because I am Your child and a joint heir with Christ Jesus. I have confidence in all things; You work for the good of those who love You, who have been called according to Your purpose.

Father God, thank You that Satan is imprisoned and unable to work in my financial state of affairs. I ask You to send Your angels out to create favor over my businesses. In the authority of Jesus, I release my ministering angels over all my finances, businesses, checking accounts savings accounts, investments, retirement funds, properties, possessions, savings, inheritances, and any financial blessing I have, or I am yet to acquire. I release my ministering angels to defend and protect my finances on my behalf according to Your will.

In the precious name of Jesus I pray. Amen.

"I will give you the keys of the kingdom of heaven. Whatever you imprison, God will imprison. And whatever you set free, God will set free." (Matthew 16:19 GW)

CHAPTER 6

Praying for Yourself

Prayer is an essential part of our lives. Beginning and ending each day with prayer is something that is of enormous worth. Prayer allows us to speak to our heavenly Father on a regular basis, and it helps us build and maintain an intimate relationship with Him. We are instructed to rejoice always and pray continually, so we should pray with an attitude of dependency upon God. We are His children, heirs with Christ Jesus, and God loves all of His children. He has blessings stored up for us just for the asking. Feel good about asking your heavenly Father for any concern that you may have.

Praying for yourself will empower you to live the way God wants you to. It will also help you become more like Jesus. After all, even Jesus prayed for Himself. It is not selfish to pray for your own needs and desires. In fact, it's critical to do so because the person with the greatest authority to help or hinder God's work in your life is you.

It is essential to establish a regular time and place to pray and read the Bible every day. Make the time necessary to develop a fresh passion to pursue God's purposes for your life. Pray for specific things based on what God has already promised to do in His Word. Look for Scriptures that will help inspire your prayers and go after God's perfect plan for your life. Invite God to speak to you through His Word and pray for a passion for His truths. Have faith that a continual pursuit of Scripture will help you remain close to Jesus.

God wants to have intimate relationships with His children, and the only way for that to happen is for us to talk to Him and to listen for His response. He tells us what we ask for will be given, what we seek will be found, and when we knock, the door will be opened to us. If you have not been seeking God daily through pray, start today. Continually ask God to saturate you with the knowledge of His will through all the wisdom and understanding that the Scriptures and the Holy Spirit gives.

He is waiting to hear from you, and He desires for you to hear from Him.

Scriptures for Yourself

"Asking God, the glorious Father of our Lord Jesus Christ, to give you spiritual wisdom and insight so that you might grow in your knowledge of God." (Ephesians 1:17 NLT)

"Keep on asking, and you will receive what you ask for. Keep on seeking, and you will find. Keep on knocking, and the door will be opened to you." (Matthew 7:7 NLT)

"And we know that for those who love God all things work together for good for those who are called according to his purpose." (Romans 8:28 ESV)

"Always be joyful. Never stop praying. Be thankful in all circumstances, for this is God's will for you who belong to Christ Jesus." (1 Thessalonians 5:16-18 NLT)

"Be diligent to present yourself approved to God as a workman who does not need to be ashamed, accurately handling the word of truth." (2 Timothy 2:15 NASB)

"You were taught to change the way you were living. The person you used to be will ruin you through desires that deceive you. However, you were taught to have a new attitude. You were also taught to become a new person created to be like God, truly righteous and holy." (Ephesians 4:22-24 GW)

[15] Call upon Me in the day of trouble; I shall rescue you, and you will honor Me." Psalm 50:15 (NASB)

Prayers for Yourself

Creating a Healthy and Nurturing Environment

Dear Heavenly Father, I bow down before You and surrender myself. I realize it is beyond my ability to live right without Your help. My desire is to live in a way that is pleasing to You. I realize to do that I require Your assistance constantly. I pray You will enable me to live righteously and walk in integrity so my children are blessed, happy, fortunate, and content.

Holy Spirit, help me to be a light in the world and teach me how to love others unconditionally like God loves me. Bring me to my maturity, set me free, heal me, and make me complete. Teach me to obey God's Word and behave appropriately so that others will see my obedient examples. I pray Your beauty will be so evident in me that I will be a good role model for others. Remove from me all things that hold me back from being the kind of Christian God desires for me to be and fill me with what I lack.

Father God, I have faith that when I ask for anything that is in Your will, in the name of Jesus, I shall receive it. I ask that You will increase my faith and give me wisdom, discernment, revelation, guidance, patience, and strength. Give me the skills, words, and perseverance that I need to nurture those around me. Instruct me how to truly intercede for others. I have a desire to attend to the things that You put on my heart to pray about concerning others needs.

In the precious name of Jesus I pray. Amen.

"You are light for the world. A city cannot be hidden when it is located on a hill." (Matthew 5:14 GW)

Wise Words Bring Healing

Father God, I am grateful that Your Word brings health and healing into every situation. I pray You will make me more like You so that my words bring comfort and encouragement to everyone around me. It is my desire for the words of my mouth and the meditation of my heart to be pleasing in Your sight. I realize that reckless words pierce like a sword; however, the tongue of the wise brings healing. Therefore a tongue that brings healing is a tree of life but a deceitful tongue crushes the spirit.

Father God, I believe that the mouth of the righteous utter wisdom and their tongues speak what is just. I choose to speak life, health, and prosperity into the lives of the ones I love. I pray You will set a guard over my mouth and keep a watch over the door of my lips. Help me to have patience with others, to be quick to listen and slow to speak.

Holy Spirit, encourage me to speak pleasant words that are like a honeycomb, sweet to the soul and healing to the bones. I give You permission to speak through me. I give You control over my tongue and my words. When I am not speaking positively, get my attention so that I can change my words for the glory of God.

In the precious name of Jesus I pray. Amen.

"Some people make cutting remarks, but the words of the wise bring healing." (Proverbs 12:18 NLT)

Humbled in the Lord's Presence

Father God, I realize I am made out of dust and I am a sinner. Please be merciful to me. I humble myself and pray, seeking Your presence. I choose to turn my back from my sinful ways. I have faith that You are listening from heaven, forgiving my sins, and restoring my health. I desire to depart from my pride. I recognize my sinful nature is full of self-centeredness, self-indulgence, and self-love.

Father God, help me to remember that Your strength is perfected in my weakness and when I choose to humble myself, I will have victory with my faults. Forgive me for depending upon my own strength and not Yours. Help me decrease so that You can increase in me. It is my desire to be obedient to Your guidance and wisdom. I want to live in

Your presence, pure in heart and action, living the life You set before me.

Father God, I have faith that I will always be Your child because You have given to me the same covenant guarantees You gave to my forefathers. I am certain that Your name is stamped on me forever and that Your eyes are always watching me. I have faith that You will stand behind me, making me a sure thing on a solid foundation.

Father God, I am positive You desire for me to have a humble heart and a contrite spirit. I understand that true humility requires me to empty myself and be filled with You. I acknowledge that I am Your creation, and I yield to Your rightful place over my life. I believe with total humility and surrender I will discover the intimacy of Your presence.

In the precious name of Jesus I pray. Amen.

"Humble yourselves in the Lord's presence. Then he will give you a high position." (James 4:10 GWT)

Kingdom Assignments

Father God, I pray that You will release me into the ministry positions that You have planned for me from the foundation of this world. Use me mightily for Your kingdom and give me divine ordained encounters and favor with everyone I meet. I pray You will open doors of opportunity that no man can shut and close the doors in my life that are not in Your will.

Holy Spirit, encourage me to look ahead and not behind. Give me dreams, visions, and discernment of God's Word and His will. Encourage me to be accessible and responsive to the request from heaven. I desire to always seek God's approval in all that I do and live for His kingdom's assignments.

Heavenly Father, I am certain that You know the plans that You have for me, plans to give me hope and a future. Thank You for those plans and for Your unconditional love and the abundant blessings that You shower down on me. I realize that Your divine steps for me may include battles and things that will be heartbreaking. I also understand that Your ways are not my ways and Your thoughts are not my thoughts. They are more than I could ever have hoped for or imagined. I am grateful that You comfort me in my troubles and in the end I will experience victory.

Father God, I believe that You are constantly planning heavenly relationships, divine encounters, and appointments for me. You are joining me with the people I need and the people who need me. I have faith You are leading me to the resources that I have been looking for so I can accomplish the kingdom assignments You have designed for me. I will walk in confidence, knowing that Your ways include a wide assortment of people and tools, and in Your timing, You will bring about Your loving plan for me.

Father God, I am certain that You know all my struggles and reservations, and You are working to help me grow, even when I can't see it. You know exactly what You are doing, and I trust Your plans. I realize that there is something bigger going on than I can understand. I am convinced You are shaping my life into something very beautiful and precious. I declare that You are the light on my path and You will keep Your promises in the days when I can't see where I am going.

In the precious name of Jesus I pray. Amen.

"And he said unto them, Let us go into the next towns that I may preach there also: for therefore came I forth." (Mark 1:38 KJV)

His Strength for My Weakness

Heavenly Father, I totally surrender my life into Your loving arms. I lay down my life into Your mighty hands. I realize that You know what is best for me. I believe that You have already considered my every need and You know my beginning from my end.

Lord Jesus, I place my trust in You. I realize that my spirit is willing but that my flesh is weak. Help me to watch and pray so that I will not fall into temptation. Strengthen me to be joyful always, to pray continually, and to give thanks in all circumstances. I believe this is God's will for me. I pray You will show me what to pray about in every situation.

Father God, thank You for guiding me through the tough years of my life. Without Your faithful unconditional love and protection, I never would have made it. I am grateful for Your angels that surround me, for the hedge of protection that covers me, and for the blood of Jesus that saved me. It is a comfort to know that You are always right by my side, supporting me and giving me courage and strength throughout my weakness.

Father God, I realize that time and again You have better things in store for me than an immediate answer to my prayer. I am confident Your grace will appear if the answer does not come, and Your grace will be of greater value to me than the direct answer to my prayer. I walk in confidence, knowing that Your grace is sufficient for me and Your power is made perfect in my weakness. Therefore, I will boast all the more gladly about my weaknesses so that Christ's power may rest on me.

In the precious name of Jesus I pray. Amen.

"Keep watching and praying that you may not enter into temptation; the spirit is willing, but the flesh is weak." (Matthew 26:41 NASB)

Yielding to God's Will

Father God, I declare from this day forward I relinquish all I have to You. I will die to myself by giving my life to You daily. I will let the Holy Spirit lead my steps. I give my desires, hopes, fears, dreams, troubles, and needs to You completely. I yield entirely to Your will. Please take my good and bad, all that I am. I choose to live for You all the days of my life. I am making Your kingdom my primary concern.

Father God, I am yielding my will to Your will because it is my hope to achieve a humble and reverent spirit. I declare that my body is the Holy Spirit's temple. I will yield my entire body to You as an instrument of righteousness. I pray You will soak my mind with Your wisdom, and create a new heart in me, and put a fresh and humble spirit in me.

Father God, thank You for receiving my humble and repentant heart. I believe that sincerity toward You and trust in You are what You require. I have faith that my Lord Jesus abides in my innermost being with all His splendor and authority. I pray as I increase in the gifts of the Holy Spirit, and practice the likeness of Jesus Christ. I will mature in my prayer, praise, and worship time.

Father God, I love You with all my heart, mind, soul, and strength. I turn all that I have over to You. I seek to be in Your will, in Your presence, and in an intimate relationship with You. I have faith that You will continue to give me the joy and peace that comes from Your salvation. I am humbled by Your mighty power. I am certain when I yield to Jesus I am on the threshold of some of the greatest victories of my life.

In the precious name of Jesus I pray. Amen.

"Do not present your members to sin as instruments for unrighteousness, but present yourselves to God as those who have been brought from death to life, and your members to God as instruments for righteousness." (Romans 6:13 ESV)

My Marriage Is Blessed

Father God, I pray that You will bless our marriage and it will always align with Your will. I declare we are one in Christ and His anointing is on our marriage. I have faith You have joined us together and no one can separate us or defeat us. I proclaim our marriage is blessed and we will spend the rest of our long healthy, happy, prosperous, lives together serving, worshipping, and praising You.

Heavenly Father, we choose to sow seeds of love in our marriage, as a result we will receive an abundant harvest of blessings. We resolve to love each other as Christ loves the church by giving each other first place and consideration in all that we do. We choose to love one another deeply because we know love covers a multitude of sins.

Father God, I proclaim that we avoid anger, bitterness, and strife at all cost. We choose to be kind and compassionate to one another, forgiving each other just as You forgave us. We will not allow corrupt statements but only what is good and edifying to come from our mouths. I adore my (husband/wife) and speak well of (him/her) to others. I choose to encourage my (husband/wife) in (his/her) walk of faith so that my words minister grace. I speak kindly to (him/her) and give (him/her) the honor, respect, and kindness that (he/she) deserves.

Father God, I declare that as we increase in the knowledge of You, our marriage is made stronger. We stand together in faith and declare that alone we can put one thousand to flight. Therefore, when my (husband/wife) and I agree, we can put ten thousands to flight. For that reason, we made the decision to stand in agreement, and we behold constant victory over our lives.

Father God, I am confident because we choose to serve You, our lives are redeemed from destruction and no weapon formed against us shall prosper. I declare that we will renew our minds in the Word daily. We are obedient to Your commands so our days shall be long, and we will have peace, and wholeness in our marriage. I have confidence there is nothing missing, lacking, or broken in our marriage.

Father God, thank You for blessing me with such an incredible (man/women) of God, I believe I was created to be a suitable helpmate for (him/her). I have confidence (he/she) is faithful to me because everything that (he/she) needs and desires is in me. I am positive that a man who finds a wife finds a good thing and he obtains favor from the Lord. I declare that a godly wife is benefit and not a burden to her husband and he can trust in her me for wise counsel.

Holy Spirit, I declare that our family is in God's perfect will because He is a lamp onto our feet and a light for our path. He guides us with wisdom, and we have the power to obtain wealth. I declare God provides abundantly for our every need. I declare that we handle money wisely and we are loyal to pay our tithes and offerings because of this, the windows of heaven remain open over our lives. I declare as for me and my house we will serve Jesus.

In the precious name of Jesus I pray. Amen.

"Let all bitterness, wrath, anger, clamor, and evil speaking be put away from you, with all malice. And be kind to one another, tenderhearted, forgiving one another, even as God in Christ forgave you." (Ephesians 4:31-2 NKJV)

All to Jesus I Surrender

Father God, I choose to pursue You with all that I have within me. I desire to know You intimately and understand You more each day. I declare that I will live for You all the days of my life. I lift up my hands and my heart. I surrender completely to You because I love You with all my heart, all my soul, and all my strength. I am thankful that my disobedience cannot live in Your almighty presence. I choose to let go of my self-centered will and collapse into Your loving arms.

Holy Spirit, equip me to obey God's Word. My spirit is willing; however, my flesh is often weak. I consent to let You stir within me both the strength and the passion to totally surrender. Purify my heart, mind, soul, and speech, and cleanse my conscious and subconscious thoughts. Capture my every thought and make every thought imprisoned that doesn't conform to Christ's standards. Help me to evaluate every one of my actions, desires, and impulses and bring everything under the control of Jesus.

Lord Jesus, I confess that my body is the Holy Spirit's temple, for that reason I offer my body as a living sacrifice, holy and pleasing to God. I have confidence this is true worship. I choose to die to myself as I lay my burdens at Your feet. I give my plans, worries, dreams, and needs to You completely. I cannot endure carrying them on my own.

Heavenly Father, I pray You will perform Your good and perfect plan in my life. I am Your servant to do with as You wish. I put all my trust in You because I believe in Your Word completely. I am grateful You take care of me. I consent to anything that You ask. I am humbled before You. I give You glory and praise. I place my future in Your hands.

Gracious Heavenly Father, I yield and surrender my life to my Lord and Savior, who gave His life so that I could live, and to the Holy Spirit, who gives me comfort, encouragement, and wisdom. I desire for Jesus to live in me with all His beauty and power. I long for my life to be a reflection of Jesus. I hand over everything I control regardless of the cost.

Lord Jesus, I am certain when I totally surrender to You and make the kingdom of God my primary concern. I can stand alongside You victoriously in battle. For that reason, I choose to surrender all that I am to You and clothe myself with the complete armor of God.

Lord Jesus, I choose to put on the girdle of truth so I can stand firm in the certainty of Your Word. I choose to put on the breastplate of righteousness so I can guard my heart from wickedness. I choose to put on the shoes of peace so I can move forward with the good news of the gospel. I choose to hold on to the shield of faith so I will be ready for the Enemies fiery darts of deceit and accusation. I choose to put on the helmet of salvation so I can keep my mind concentrated on You. I choose to pick up the double-edged sword of the spirit of Your Word so it will be ready in my hands.

In the precious name of Jesus I pray. Amen.

"Brothers and sisters, because of God's compassion toward us, I encourage you to offer your bodies as living sacrifices, dedicated to God and pleasing to him. This kind of worship is appropriate for you." (Romans 12:1 GW)

Spiritual Hunger

Father God, I hunger for Your touch. My soul thirsts for You, the true living God. I aspire to be in Your Word and in Your favor constantly. I am confident as I seek Your presence and delight myself in You, You will give me the desires of my heart.

Heavenly Father, I pray that every choice that I make will be filled with love and reverence towards You. If there is ever a moment that I am walking out of Your reach, remind me that there is a heaven and a hell and that there are consequences for my choices. Help me remember that I have the choice of life and death and living for my flesh and worldly things will cause spiritual death.

Holy Spirit, create in me a teachable spirit. Remove from me the spirit of "I am right" and replace it with a spirit of "I want to gain knowledge." Please guide me by God's truth and help me to pray passionately and listen in silence and solitude. It is my desire to be joyful always and to pray continually. I have an eagerness to become a prayer warrior.

Father God, I pray I will have the courage to do what You tell me to. I pray that I will hear Your voice and my strength will be renewed and refreshed daily. Eliminate from my heart any distractions that are keeping me from You. Take away any ungodliness from my life and let all that resists You unsettle me. I want to be drawn to things that are full of Your love and light.

Father God, I pray that my daily walk with You will burn with an unwavering spiritual hunger for divine things. I declare that I will say yes to the things of Your will and no to the things of the flesh. Engrave Your laws upon my heart and mind so that I will walk with confidence and assurance in the righteousness of Your commands.

Lord Jesus, as a deer longs for flowing streams of water so my soul longs for You. My soul thirsts for the living God. I desire to see Your face and to meet with You frequently. I need You like a newborn baby needs milk. I ask for discernment and understanding. I earnestly seek out knowledge of Your will. It is my desire to listen for Your whisper as I search Your Word diligently for wisdom.

In the precious name of Jesus I pray. Amen.

"As a deer longs for flowing streams, so my soul longs for you, O God. My soul thirsts for God, for the living God. When may I come to see God's face?" (Psalm 42:1-2 GW)

Change Me into the Likeness of Christ

Heavenly Father, the love I have for You is stronger than my love for anyone or anything else. I choose to hide Your Word in my heart so that I might not sin against You. I desire for my heart to be pure, my motives to be holy, and my reflection to be of Jesus Christ. I declare that I will seek Jesus wholeheartedly, giving Him first place and consideration in all that I do. I am certain when I live this way I am blessed and I shall see Your glorious face.

Holy Spirit, help me to do what is right. Teach me to respect and understand God's laws. Remind me that they are there for my benefit and when I am not following them; my life will end up in disorder. I desire to be drawn to what pleases God, and I want to run away from ungodly or evil things.

Heavenly Father, open my eyes and my heart and let me sense Your anointing. I pray You will transform me into the likeness of Christ. I am confident when I exhibit my new life in Christ, a life that is refreshed every day, I will grow in my understanding of Jesus and becoming more and more like Him. I have faith as a believer I partake of Jesus' divine nature and have the power to live for You victoriously.

Father God, I pray You will examine me and search me. Look closely into my heart and mind Purify me and bring me to true repentance. I believe that living in purity brings life, holiness, and blessings. I declare that I am more than a conqueror through Jesus, who lives in me, and there is no condemnation for those who are in Christ Jesus. I proclaim that I will not walk according to the flesh but according to the Holy Spirit.

In the precious name of Jesus I pray. Amen.

"Do not lie to one another, seeing that you have put off the old self with its practices and have put on the new self, which is being renewed in knowledge after the image of its creator." (Colossians 3:9-10 ESV)

Create in Me a Pure Heart

Heavenly Father, You are my God, and I earnestly seek and thirst for You. As Your child, I come humbly yet boldly before Your throne of mercy and grace. I am so grateful that I have the benefit of crawling up into Your lap and feeling Your loving arms around me. I pray that I will hear Your quiet whisper, and I can sit in silences long enough not too miss Your voice.

Father God, I declare I am Your handiwork, created in Christ Jesus to do the good work that You prepared in advance for me. I long for the characteristic of Jesus to be produced in me through the Holy Spirit's empowerment. I welcome the Holy Spirit in all areas of my life. I dedicate my entire body as a living sacrifice. I declare that my heart is a temple of Your Holy Spirit. I long for love, joy, peace, patience, kindness, goodness, faithfulness, gentleness, and self-control to flow out of me.

Holy Spirit, help me to see more clearly. Open the eyes of my heart and reveal to me what changes I need to make in my life that I may not realize. I desire for Your cleansing living water to flow through my innermost being. I realize I must reach a point where I am willing to see the sharp edges that I have on me. I release my bad attitudes, perceptions, viewpoints, fears, worries, selfishness, and desires into Your capable hands.

Lord Jesus, I pray You will create in me a pure heart and renew a right spirit within me. Dwell in me today and cleanse me from my sins from first to last. Give me the courage to see and admit my sins as part of my sinful nature that is weak and wicked. Give me the strength to repent of them.

In the precious name of Jesus I pray. Amen.

"Create in me a clean heart, O God, and renew a right spirit within me." (Psalm 51:10 ESV)

Asking and Receiving

Heavenly Father, my faith grows by knowing that without a doubt I am able to ask You for anything I lack; and You are the only one who can meet those needs. I come boldly into Your throne of grace too obtain mercy and find miracle to help in my time of need. I have faith if I ask for anything I desire that is according to Your will in the name of Jesus, I shall receive it.

Gracious Heavenly Father, I am grateful for the promises that when I ask, it shall be given, when I seek, I shall find, and when I knock, the door shall be open. For that reason I ask for wisdom and guidance. I pray that I will find You when I seek You with my whole heart. I pray I will only knock on doors that You want opened for me.

Father God, I confess that You know the plans that You have for me, plans to give me a hope and a future. I pray You will give me strength and guide me down a safe path. Show me the way that I should go. When I wander off the road to the left or to the right, I believe that I will hear Your voice behind me, saying, "This is the way. Follow Me." I pray as I seek You I will hear a clear answer from You in all areas of my life. I pray You will instruct, guide, and protect me.

Father God, I ask You to train me in wisdom to do Your will. I ask for Your prefect will to be done in my life so that my joy will be complete. I have faith that You will give me the desires of my heart. Thank You for the desires You have placed in me. I desire for Your will to be done in my life. I want to please You in all my words, activities, and actions. I desire to have ears to hear You and eyes to see You. Open my eyes to see Your vision for my life and my ears to hear Your voice.

In the precious name of Jesus I pray. Amen.

"If you ask me anything in my name, I will do it." (John 14:14 ESV)

Delight Yourself in the Lord

Father God, I am so grateful that You have placed the desires of my heart in me. I am certain that those desires are revealed to me and manifested in me when I delight myself in You. I am convinced that You search my heart and understand every motive behind my thoughts. I desire for Your prefect will to be done in me. I want to please You in all my, conduct, conversations, and dealings.

Heavenly Father, I pray for understanding and direction. Please instruct me to do Your will. Guide me down a safe path and show me the way that I should go. I have confidence that You instruct, guide, and protect those who please You. My desire is to only knock on doors that You want opened for me.

Father God, I am convinced that I will find You when I seek You with my whole heart. I have faith that when I put my total trust and focus on You, You will provide me with everything I need. I declare that You are my foundation, my provider, and my creator. I trust that Your will has no limits and Your observation sees every possibility. I believe Your willingness to invest in me is unrestricted and Your readiness to grant me success is always immediate.

Father God, I confess that You know the plans that You have for me, plans to prosper me. I believe the heart of Your will is a never-ending love for me, and a relentless desire to bless me. I have faith that when Your will is accomplished, the results are amazing. I am grateful that You know me so well and You can provide for the best outcomes in every situation.

Holy Spirit, I desire to hear and see in the heavenly realm. I pray as I delight myself in God I will gain wisdom, understanding, and knowledge. I believe at the center of every conversation I have with God is an opportunity to delight myself in Him.

In the precious name of Jesus I pray. Amen.

"Delight yourself in the Lord, and he will give you the desires of your heart." (Psalm 37:4 ESV)

My Shepherd

Dear Lord, I proclaim that You are my shepherd, and I shall not want. You provide for all my needs. Before I ask, You answer. You make me lie down in green pasture. You lead me besides quiet waters, and You restore my soul. You give me peace when I am weary and restoration when I am weak. You guide me in the path of righteousness for Your namesake. You keep me on the road You have ordained for me.

Father God, when I walk through the valley of the shadow of death, I will fear no evil, for You are with me. You give Your angels charge over me to protect me when danger is near. Your rod and Your staff, they comfort me. You are my comfort and my shield, my ever-present help in time of trouble.

Father God, You prepare a table before me in the presence of my enemies. You proclaim Your love on me for everyone to see. You anoint my head with oil, and my cup overflows. I am so thankful that You shower Your love on me, and I have more that I need.

Heavenly Father, I declare that goodness and love will follow me all the days of my life because I am blessed beyond measure. I will dwell in Your house forever, and I will serve You all of my days.

In the precious name of Jesus I pray. Amen.

The Lord is my Shepherd: (Psalm 23 GW)

Eternal Encouragement

Father God, I am certain I can boldly enter heaven before Your throne of grace and mercy and fall at Your feet. I choose to worship and pray to You because You are my greatest encourager. I declare that Jesus came to reveal that You are for me, not against me and to tell me You are not counting my sins. I have full assurance of faith that You call me to persevere no matter what while I am here on earth. I have no doubt You encourage me to be strong and courageous so I will not be anxious about anything. I am certain You accompany me and will not leave me or forsake me.

Holy Spirit, I am so grateful that Jesus loves me, and gives me eternal encouragement, and hope by His grace. God's word has given me faith that I am not alone in this fight against the Enemy. I am indebted to God's mercy, strength, support, and encouragement that He offers to me so freely. I am certain He wants me to remain positive as He guides me in my Christian journey.

Father God, Your encouragement makes all the difference to me. I am grateful for Your generous words of assurance and comfort in my times of troubles. When I am brokenhearted, You are close to me like a shepherd who carries a lamb. You have carried me close to Your heart. I am thankful that one day You will wipe away every tear from my eyes and take away all the pain I have suffered on this earth.

In the precious name of Jesus I pray. Amen.

"God our Father loved us and by his kindness gave us everlasting encouragement and good hope. Together with our Lord Jesus Christ, may he encourage and strengthen you to do and say everything that is good." (2 Thessalonians 2:16-17 GW)

My Hope Is in the Lord

Father God, I will praise You forever for all You have done. I place all my hope in You. You are the God of hope and I trust in Your name. I believe You delight in those who fear You, those who put their hope in Your unfailing love. I declare my heart is satisfied, my tongue rejoices, and my body rests in anticipation of Your overflowing hope by the power of the Holy Spirit.

Holy Spirit, I choose to place all my hope and trust only in God. I have been justified through faith, and I have peace and hope in God through my Lord Jesus Christ. I am certain I have gained access by faith into this grace in which I now stand, and I boast in the hope of the glory of God.

Heavenly Father, I am confident in what I hope for and assured about what I do not see. The path I walk is one of ultimate trust in You. I am convinced that You are on my side, guiding and protecting me all the way on my journey in good times and in bad times.

Father God, I declare You are my God and my Savior and all my hope remains in You. I will be strong and take heart since You are my refuge and my shield. I pray You will guide me in Your truth and teach me Your ways so that I can walk in Your truth. Create in me an undivided heart so that I discern how to fear Your name.

In the precious name of Jesus I pray. Amen.

"You are my hiding place and my shield. My hope is based on your word." (Psalm 119:114 GW)

Move Me into the Purpose I Was Created For

Father God, I believe that a man's heart plans his ways but that You direct his steps. I pray that You will encourage me in Your ways and lead me down a smooth path, move me into the purpose I was created for. Guide me down the path that You have designed for me. I have faith that You know exactly what You are doing. I trust Your plans, even though I can't see the final results. I believe that You are making my life into something beautiful and valuable. I have faith that there is always something better happening than what I can see.

Heavenly Father, I declare I will not to be anxious about anything; however I will bring everything to You in prayer and petition with thanksgiving. I know You are here with me at this very moment, and You are faithful, and You will use this prayer for Your purpose.

Holy Spirit, I am grateful God shows me the way along unfamiliar paths. When I am blinded by this world, He guides me, and turns my darkness into light before me; He makes my rough places smooth. I am certain that God will never forsake me. I pray I will recognize God's soft whisper, and You will remind me that every encounter is for the glory and purposes of God. I am convinced that the people who cross my path are there at that very moment to accomplish God's perfect plan.

Father God, every day You teach me to trust You, to recognize that life is a journey filled with gates to open and trails to be cleared, and many things of which I will not understand. I put all my trust in Your divine way of thinking. I realize my life will include steps forward, and steps back with victories, and disappointments, and maybe even some unclear path. However, even during the days when I can't see where I am going, I have faith in Your promises.

In the precious name of Jesus I pray. Amen.

"I will lead the blind by ways they have not known, along unfamiliar paths I will guide them; I will turn the darkness into light before them and make the rough places smooth. These are the things I will do; I will not forsake them." (Isaiah 42:16 NIV)

The Lamb's Book of Life

Father God, thank you for Your generosity. I am so grateful that through faith in Jesus, I have access to You by the Holy Spirit. I realize it is only by Your grace and mercy that my name is written in heaven. I have faith that Jesus offered me eternal life when I trusted Him as my Lord and Savior. I am certain for that reason only my name is written in the Lamb's book of life.

Father God, I rejoice that through Jesus, Your one and only Son, I have been given eternal life so that I may know You, the only true God. I am confident that from the first moment I trusted Christ, my body was dead because of sin, yet my spirit became alive because of righteousness. Therefore, I count myself dead to sin but alive in Christ Jesus. I am so grateful, that Jesus lives in me, and I am no longer controlled by my sinful nature.

Heavenly Father, I understand that the wages of sin is death but that the gift of God is eternal life in my Lord and Savior. I have faith that I have freedom from my entire past because who the Son sets free is free indeed. As a result, everyone who is in Christ, they are a new creation. The old is gone, and the new has come.

Holy Spirit, help me to stay pure at heart, honorable, and truthful in all that I do. I am certain that nothing impure and no one who does what is shameful or deceitful will enter heaven. Only those whose names are written in the Lamb's book of life will be allowed entrance.

In the precious name of Jesus I pray. Amen.

"Nothing impure will ever enter it, nor will anyone who does what is shameful or deceitful, but only those whose names are written in the Lamb's book of life." (Revelation 21:27 NIV)

Trusting in My Light and My Salvation

Father God, I trust in Your unfailing love, and my heart rejoices in Your salvation. I declare You are my light and my salvation, so I shall not fear. You are the stronghold in my life. I shall not be afraid. You alone are my rock and my salvation, my fortress in times of trouble. I have faith that I will never be shaken because I have victory in Jesus.

Heavenly Father, I believe You saved me for Your namesake to make Your mighty power known. I am grateful that when I am weak, You restore me and make Your face shine upon me so that I am free from any harmful influences that stalk me. I understand that by myself, I cannot hold my own against the spiritual forces of darkness; however, You are the authority of my life. You are my protection, my support, and my refuge. I trust Your faithfulness, and rely on Your loyalty, and dependability.

Father God, I proclaim You are my light and my salvation. I declare I fearlessly trust in You. You deliver me from my spiritual enemies and rescue me from the punishment I deserve for my sins. I realize that I am human and that I am weak and vulnerable, easily crushed and broken physically, emotionally, and spiritually. I realize it is only by Your grace and mercy that I have become Your child. Thank You for allowing the Holy Spirit to enter my life to comfort, guide and counsel me. I am confident when my earthly life is over, I will spend eternity in heaven with You.

In the precious name of Jesus I pray. Amen.

"The Lord is my light and my salvation. Who is there to fear? The Lord is my life's fortress. Who is there to be afraid of?" (Psalm 27:1 GW)

Resting in the Father's Love

Father God, I am grateful that You have always been my Father. I am confident You will always be my Father. Thank You for giving me the precious gift of Your love and for showing me what true love looks like. I will forever rest in Your love. I remind myself You request nothing more than the simple trusting heart of a child.

Father God, I realize there is no human experience that I might walk through where Your love can not reach me. If I climb the highest mountain, You are there, and yet if I find myself in the darkest valley of my life, You are there. I am convinced that death or life, angels or demons, the present or the future, height or depth, or any powers or anything else in all creation will be able to separate me from the love I have found in Christ Jesus.

Father God, I am certain You gave up everything You loved so that I might gain Your love. I am certain when I received the gift of Your Son, Jesus, I received Your love. I believe that Jesus is the exact likeness of You and that in Jesus, Your love for me is revealed. I have faith that You love me even as You love Jesus. I realize Jesus died so that I could reconcile with You. His death was the ultimate expression of Your love for me.

Father God, I am so grateful that nothing will ever separate me from Your love. I take comfort in knowing that You are my shepherd and I shall not want. You provide for all my needs, keeping me safe from predators and guiding me away from danger. I have faith that no power on earth or in heaven could separate me from Your love, not my sin, not any authority, not any spiritual force. I trust that Your love is unshakable and that I can always rely upon it.

In the precious name of Jesus I pray. Amen.

"For I am convinced that neither death, nor life, nor angels, nor principalities, nor things present, nor things to come, nor powers, nor height, nor depth, nor any other created thing, will be able to separate us from the love of God, which is in Christ Jesus our Lord." (Romans 8:38-9 NASB)

A Treasured Possession

Father God, thank You for calling me Your own and for having Your hand on my life. I declare I am Your treasured possession, because You called my name, and drew me close to You. Then You set me apart and called me holy. I am certain that as Your treasured possession, You take care of my every need. You cherish and adore me, and love me unconditionally with a love which endures forever. I am convinced I never leave Your sight and I am always on Your mind.

Heavenly Father, I am certain You are the complete expression of love and You love me with an everlasting love. Thank You for providing me with more than my earthly father ever could. I believe that it is Your desire to lavish Your love on me simply because I am Your child and You are the perfect Father. I am so grateful that You are familiar with everything about me. You know when I sit down and when I rise up, You know all my ways.

Father God, I believe I was made in Your image, and in You, I live, move, and have my existence. I am Your child and You determined the exact time of my birth and where I would live. I am certain before I was conceived, You knew me. You chose me when You designed creation. For that reason I am fearfully and wonderfully made. You knitted me together in my mother's womb. You brought me forth on the day that I was born and numbered the very hairs on my head.

Father God, I realize that every perfect gift that I receive comes from Your mighty hands. I proclaim that You are my Jehovah Jireh. You meet all my needs according to Your glorious riches through Christ Jesus, not by my ability. I am certain Your plan for my future has always been abundantly spilling over with blessings and miracles.

Father God, I believe Your thoughts toward me are beyond measure like the sands on the seashores. I have faith that You are always moving all around me and You will never stop doing excellent things for me. I trust that You rejoice over me with singing and that You dance over me when I am unaware.

In the precious name of Jesus I pray. Amen.

"For you are a people holy to the Lord your God, and the Lord has chosen you to be a people for his treasured possession, out of all the peoples who are on the face of the earth." (Deuteronomy 14:2 ESV)

Grace and Mercy, the Gifts of God

Heavenly Father, thank You for giving me the privilege to experience Your grace and mercy through the forgiveness of my sins. I have faith that it is by grace that I have been saved through faith. I realize I did not achieve my own salvation. It is a gift from You. I acknowledge that

Jesus is the way, the truth, and the life and no one can come to You except through Jesus.

Father God, I believe that Jesus is grace Himself, grace in the flesh, and the grace of Jesus encourages me to change my outlook of myself and my awareness of Your purpose for me. I believe that through the riches of Your grace, the blood of Jesus, and the forgiveness of my sins, I have received redemption. I declare I have been justified through faith and I have peace through my Lord and Savior Jesus Christ.

Father God, I declare that Your grace is sufficient in all my circumstances. Knowing that Your grace and mercy is at work in me is my greatest source of comfort. I am grateful that my relationship with You is not based on my performance or good works but on my faith. I understand that there is no condemnation for those who are in Christ Jesus.

Father God, every day, I count on Your grace, the grace that restored me and the grace that unshackled my life. I declare from the fullness of Your grace, I have received one blessing after another, for that reason I am encouraged in my walk of faith. I take comfort in knowing that Your grace furnishes what is lacking as a result of my personal weakness.

Gracious Father God, I believe that it is Your grace that makes us disciples, and Your grace, and mercy is available to all who choose to trust Jesus as their Savior. I am certain that by means of grace I have received the promise of the Holy Spirit. I pray that the power of the Holy Spirit will increase in me as I grow in the grace and knowledge of Jesus Christ.

In the precious name of Jesus I pray. Amen.

"For by grace you have been saved through faith. And this is not your own doing; it is the gift of God." (Ephesians 2:8 ESV)

Finding Peace, Position, Provision, Privilege, and Victory

Father God, in the name of Jesus, I claim peace, position, provision, privilege, and victory over my life. I declare I will fear not, for You are with me and I am with You. I trust that my whole life is established in my intimate relationship with You. I depend on You as my Heavenly Father, my Lord and Savior, and my good and faithful friend.

Holy Spirit, thank You for the personal inner peace that surpasses all understanding that You gave to me when my life was full of turmoil. I declare that grace and peace are mine in abundances through the knowledge of my Lord Jesus. His peace guards my heart and mind as I live in Him. I have faith that His peace will satisfy me because Jesus is the Prince of Peace. He gives peace and rest to all who come to Him in faith.

Father God, I am confident as Your child, You call me Your beloved and set me in my heavenly position. I declare that I am raised up to my heavenly position, and I will step up to serve Jesus each day. I will continue His work in this world so that my hands will give away what He came to give. I believe that what Jesus started He has left for His followers to carry on. I believe that I am the hands, feet, and mouth of Jesus. I have faith that You have set me in precise positions in my life to bless the people around me.

Holy Spirit, help me not to be so fixated on what I don't have and miss the unexpected ways God provides those very needs. Remind me to not become anxious about whether or not I have what I need. Help me to see that with God as my heavenly Father, worry is uncalled for. I declare that all the provisions I require will be available when I need them. I am convinced that everything I need will happen at once and everywhere I look, I will see blessings, blessings like wine pouring off the mountains and hills. I declare God shall supply all my needs according to His riches in glory through Christ Jesus.

Father God, thank You for the privileges that are a result of Your grace. The privileges of salvation, to enter into an intimate and eternal relationship with You. For the privilege to serve You with good works, which You perform through me. For the privilege to eat bread at Your table continually. I ask for more than enough of Your overflowing benefits. For the privilege to live an adventure of what life is like when all I have is faith in You. I have faith that what I need for tomorrow is as good as already in my hands.

Lord Jesus, I declare when it is You that I surrender to, surrender doesn't mean I give up. It means that I am on the threshold of some of the greatest victories of my life. I have faith that I will overcome with victory, no matter how intense my battles, no matter how weary I become, and no matter how overwhelming my odds. I declare I will not retreat. With the Word of God in my hand and with You fighting for me, it won't be me who retreats. I declare victory over the Enemy he has been defeated in all areas of my life.

In the precious name of Jesus I pray. Amen.

"Everything will be happening at once and everywhere you look blessings! Blessings like wine pouring off the mountains and hills." (Amos 9:13 MSG)

Enjoying the Journey with Christ

Father God, I have faith when I pour out my deepest feelings to You and pray in Your will, I will receive answers to my prayers. I pray that You will give me the wisdom to wait on Your timing. You are my hiding place; You protect me from trouble, and surround me with songs of deliverance. You instruct me and teach me in the way I should go and counsel me with Your loving eye on me.

Holy Spirit, I declare You are my helper and I will not fear what man can do to me. Thank You for the strength You give me as I walk through my journey with Christ. I cast all my fear onto God, because I know that He cares for me. I have faith when the Enemy comes, God will lift up a standard against him and sweep away the Enemy and his works.

Lord Jesus, I realize life on earth is temporary, so I humble myself under Your mighty hands. I choose to acknowledge You in all my ways. I have faith that You will direct my steps. It is my desire to truly learn more about You and understand You while I follow You. As I look back at where I was before I started with You, I can see how far I have come. I acknowledge that You have brought me this far. I have faith that You will take me the rest of the way.

Heavenly Father, I pray for the strength and wisdom to look up more than I look ahead or behind. I realize if I focus on how far I have to go, I may get discouraged. I also realize the past will not get me to the future You have planned for me.

Father God, I pray that You will bring people into my life who will mentor me and You will remove the people who hinder me. I believe that You have so much to teach me and so many teachers You want to use. I truly desire to learn more about You. Your Word is so powerful that it can transform every life. I will mediate on Your Word night and day as I walk through my journey with You.

In the precious name of Jesus I pray. Amen.

"You are my hiding place. You protect me from trouble. You surround me with joyous songs of salvation. Selah the Lord says, 'I will instruct you. I will teach you the way that you should go. I will advise you as my eyes watch over you." (Psalm 32:7-8 GW)

Prepare Me to Be a True Worshiper

Father God, I love Your name and rejoice in You. I am glad and will forever sing for joy, while I walk in the light of Your presence. You have never forsaken those who seek after You. I pray You will spread Your protection over me, as I find refuge under the shadow of Your wings.

Father God, I declare that Your love endures forever and today is the day that You have made. I choose to rejoice and be glad in it. You have done marvelous things for me; I will celebrate and worship You all day long. I will remember Your name at night and I will praise You without end.

Father God, I have made my mind up to praise and worship You as long as I live. By lifting up my hands and declaring that You are good all the time. I rejoice in Your name all day long while I delight in You. I sing to You and proclaim Your salvation day after day. I will not turn away from You, but on the contrary, I will praise and worship You forever for what You have done in the presence of everyone.

Holy Spirit, prepare me to be a true worshiper by continuing in a right relationship with God. Renew my spirit and teach me God's way so that I can walk in the truth. It is my desire to act justly, to love mercy, and to walk humbly before My God. Give me an undivided heart so that I may fear God's name. I choose to worship God and I give thanks to Him because of His righteousness.

Father God, when I praise and worship You, it is like being in spiritual paradise. Everything melts away—anxiety, fear, confusion, and worry. I am grateful when I worship with a true heart of adoration. It has such a calming and soothing effect on my state of mind.

In the precious name of Jesus I pray. Amen.

"But let all who take refuge in you rejoice. Let them sing with joy forever. Protect them, and let those who love your name triumph in you." (Psalm 5:11 GW)

His Praise Shall Continually Come from My Lips

Father God, I proclaim You inhabit the praises of Your children. I am certain when praise is continually coming from my lips, You are magnified and Your power is released to heal, save and protect. It is undeniable that there is power in praise and that You love pure, innocent, and spontaneous praise, and worship from Your children. I declare that out of the mouth of babes and nursing infants, You have ordained strength, and with this strength, You will silence the Enemy and the Avenger.

Father God, I realize You have not ordained praise because You need it but because I need it. I declare that praises to You will always be in my mouth. The double-edged sword of Your Word I will always hold in my hand. I am certain with my praise and my words, I will chain the Devil.

Holy Spirit, encourage me to have childlike faith and give me the strength that is necessary. Grant me the concentration to listen to God's instructions so that I will not forsake His teachings. I declare that each new level of knowledge and wisdom I gain, motivates my desire to praise. The ever-increasing knowledge of God inspires an ever-increasing praise in me.

Heavenly Father, I realize that You created my innermost being. You knitted me together in the womb. For that reason, I will open my lips, and my mouth will declare Your praise. I declare that I have traded in my spirit of heaviness for a garment of praise. I will continually offer a sacrifice of praise and thanksgiving from my lips.

Father God, I praise You for the gift of Jesus. I praise You for the fact that our glorious Jesus is the risen Christ. I praise You for Your holiness, mercy, justice, and grace. I praise You for Your goodness, Your kindness, and Your salvation. I declare all creation praises Your marvelous name because You are good.

In the precious name of Jesus I pray. Amen.

"Out of the mouth of babes and nursing infants You have ordained strength, Because of Your enemies, That You may silence the enemy and the avenger." (Psalm 8:2 NKJV)

Discovering True Wisdom, Knowledge and Understanding

Heavenly Father, I respect Your rules. They give me pleasure and bring me good advice. I know that they are there to bless me and protect me. I desire to develop knowledge and understanding of Your Word. I believe You offer to share Your knowledge when I call on You. I want to be fruitful in every good work, increasing in the knowledge of You. I have faith that You will give me understanding in all things. I am certain when I lack wisdom and I ask You for clarity, You will give it to me generously.

Holy Spirit, I am convinced that the fear of the Lord is the beginning of wisdom and when I follow God's precepts, I will have good understanding. Encourage me to make the time to read the Word and to pray and worship daily. It is my desire to discover true knowledge and understanding of the will of God. I realize with an intimate relationship with God, the more understanding I will receive and the wiser I will become.

Holy Spirit, I pray that as I grow in the knowledge of God, I will purse self-control. I realize that my spirit is willing but my flesh is time and again weak. I pray You will strengthen my spirit. Reveal to me how to discern between God's will and my own. Encourage me to do what is obedient.

Father God, I believe that wisdom comes from an understanding of Your Word. It is my aspiration to be able to speak Your Word with boldness. I am convinced that understanding causes wisdom to be imparted on those who seek Your truth. I declare that Your Word is my sword and it is my desire to be spiritually sharp. I pray that You will increase my knowledge and satisfy me with wisdom and understanding for my daily decisions. I believe that without Your guidance, there's nothing to keep me from being destroyed.

Heavenly Father, I have faith it is only You who gives wisdom and from Your mouth comes knowledge and understanding. I declare that Your knowledge has strengthened me and Your wisdom will always surpass all understanding. I pray that wisdom will be given to me, and You will also bless me with wealth and riches so that I can financially support Your kingdom here on earth.

In the precious name of Jesus I pray. Amen.

"For the LORD gives wisdom, and from his mouth come knowledge and understanding." (Proverbs 2:6 NIV)

I Will Fix My Eyes on Jesus

Father God, It is my desire to sincerely absorb and speak Your Word with boldness and authority. I declare I will throw off everything that hinders me, especially the sin that so easily entangles me. I understand that the power of life and death is in my tongue, so I choose to confess that I have been crucified with Christ. I declare I no longer live but Christ lives in me. I will fix my eyes on Jesus, the author and finisher of my faith. As a result I will not grow weary or lose heart, but I will find strength in Your Word. Therefore I will run with endurance the race set before me.

Father God, I declare I will focus my entire life on exactly one thing, pursuing Christ in everything I do. I will not dwell on what I have left behind, but I will look ahead to my goal. I will not just fix my eyes on what is seen or on the temporary things because I know these things shall pass away, but I will fix my eyes on what is unseen. I have faith that what is seen is temporary and that what is unseen is eternal.

Holy Spirit, give me the peace that I need when I stray off course, Your peace that surpasses all understanding. When I am feeling defeated, encourage me to refocus my eyes away from my burdens and back on my enormous Jesus. Encourage me to focus on my remarkable Lord and Savior, who has brought me this far. Remind me that the day, on the other side of this night, will be awesome in God's light and for His glory. I am certain Jesus didn't bring me this far so that I could quit. I declare I will not just start the race, but I will finish my race strongly as Jesus did for me.

Lord Jesus, encourage me to read the Bible daily and to do what the Word proclaims. Give me revelations through prophetic visions, so I will be blessed, as I pursue God's teachings. I love You with my whole mind, my whole heart, and my whole soul. I declare that You are the goal that I pursue, so with my eyes fixed on the goal, I push on to secure the prize of God's heavenward calling.

In the precious name of Jesus I pray. Amen.

"Fixing our eyes on Jesus, the author and perfector of faith, who for the joy set before Him endured the cross, despising the shame, and has sat down at the right hand of the throne of God." (Hebrews 12:2 NASB)

Mountain-Moving Faith

Heavenly Father, I am certain without faith, it is impossible to please You because faith is the core to my spiritual journey and faith is a key to accessing a divine life. I realize that salvation is an act of faith in Jesus. I also understand that Your forgiveness is an act of grace that I did not deserve. I am thankful that everything I have ever received from You is due to Your grace, and it is unearned, undeserved, and unmerited.

Father God, I choose to stay on the journey with You through successes and failures. I have the faith and willingness to radically trust in You. I am grateful for the faith that You have given me. I believe that You give everyone a measure of faith and all I need is faith the size of a mustard seed to move mountains.

Holy Spirit, encourage me to have mountain-moving faith and remind me that I must practice it every day. Help me develop a steadfast faith that will carry me through all the ups and downs of life. Help me to understand and apply faith to my life by exercising my faith. I believe that faith is essential and of the utmost importance for every aspect of my Christian walk, and I realize without faith, I can do nothing.

Father God, I have confidence that when I ask anything in prayer that is according to Your will, while believing I shall receive it. I have faith that if I wait patiently, You will turn to me and hear my prayers. I declare that faith in You assures me of the things I expect and convinces me of the things I cannot see. I know my faith will not let me down in times of trouble, loss, uncertainty, or fear. I am convinced that my faith in You can guide me through the worst and best times in my lives.

Heavenly Father, I declare because of my victorious faith that my spiritual weapons are mighty and the authority of Jesus is far greater than the power of darkness, so the Enemy must surrender. In the name of Jesus, I command all spirits that are not the Holy Spirit to depart from my life, my family, my health, my finances, and my possessions. I command that the yoke of disease and disorders be destroyed. I have faith that You have rebuked the Devourer for my namesake and You have broken the Enemy's strongholds off of me. I have faith that You will prevent all curses that have been made against me from affecting me.

In the precious name of Jesus I pray. Amen.

"Now faith is the assurance of things hoped for, the conviction of things not seen." (Hebrews 11:1 NASB)

Taking Pleasure in God's Presence

Heavenly Father, I cry out for more of Your presence in my life. The true desire of my heart is simply to know You more intimately and to be filled continually with the joy of the Holy Spirit. I choose to delight in You, loving the things that You love and truly delighting in the things that bring You joy. I long for a deeper relationship with You, finding pleasure in the riches of Your grace.

Father God, I believe that You place my desires in my heart and those desires will be made known to me when I seek Your face and delight myself in You. I have faith You will show me the path that leads to life and Your presence will fill me with joy and pleasure forever. I have confidence that when I put my total trust and focus on You, You will provide me with everything I need in life.

Holy Spirit, instruct me to do God's will and show me the way I should go. Counsel me, watch over me, and guide me down a safe path. I have confidence that You instruct, guide, and protect those who please God. Help me avoid any kind of sin or wickedness. If I drift off the road that God has for me, put me back on the straight and narrow.

Father God, I pray I will hear a clear answer from You in all areas of my life. I confess that You know the plans that You have for me, plans to give me hope and a future. I believe I will find You because I seek You with my whole heart. I am certain when I delight and seek my happiness in You, my desires will change; they will become desires that will delight You. I believe that delighting in You means finding my contentment in Your perfection, Your friendship, and Your love.

Father God, I proclaim that You are the potter and I am the clay. Make me and mold me into the image of Jesus. I want Your will to be done in my life. I want to please You in all my words, deeds, and actions. I pray You will make me what You need me to be so that I can do Your will. I pray You will make Your will my heart's desire.

Gracious Father God, I pray as I take pleasure in Your presence, I will find discernment and direction. I ask for Your prefect will for my life. I desire to only knock on doors that You want opened for me. I pray that You give me ears to hear Your voice and eyes to see Your vision for my life.

In the precious name of Jesus I pray, Amen.

"Delight yourself in the LORD; And He will give you the desires of your heart." (Psalm 37:4 NASB)

Committed to a Life of Repentance

Father God, I realize that even when I am trying to be good, there are areas in my life that remain sinful. I pray You will bring to my attention any sins that I may be holding on to so that I can confess, repent, and renounce them. I declare I am committed to a life of repentance. I am convinced that in repentance and rest is my salvation, in quietness and trust is my strength. I am certain that when I am weak, the Holy Spirit is strong in me and that when my flesh fails, Your authority never will.

Father God, I pray that I will live a life that reflects true repentance and my heart will be prepared to quickly confess my mistakes and sins. I know that I cannot live my life perfectly; however, I will do everything in my control to live my life honorably, and when I do sin, I will acknowledge my mistakes, repent, get back up, and keep walking by faith. I have confidence that blessed are those whose transgressions are forgiven, whose sins are covered.

Heavenly Father, I am certain that You have not come to call the righteous but sinners to repentance and that You are not slow in keeping Your promises as some understand slowness. Instead, You are patient with us, not wanting anyone to perish but for everyone to come to sincere repentance. I pray the words of my mouth, the actions that I take, and the thoughts in my mind remain pleasing in Your sight.

Holy Spirit, I declare it is my desire to be filled with a spirit of integrity. I pray You will encourage me to truly regret my sins. Help me from making the same mistake over and over again and give me the strength to turn from any sinful ways. Cleanse me from my sins and iniquities. Create a new heart in me and fill me with a spirit of hope, love, joy, peace, and self-control.

Father God, I am convinced for as high as the heavens are above the earth, so great is Your love for those who fear You, and as far as the east is from the west, so far have You removed my transgressions from me. I declare that I wholeheartedly believe that You are true and just to forgive me when I confess and turn from my sins. Thank You for tossing all my confessed sins and mistakes into the sea of forgetfulness.

In the precious name of Jesus I pray. Amen.

"I have not come to call the righteous but sinners to repentance." (Luke 5:32 NASB)

The Meal that Heals and Restores

Heavenly Father, Your love is so amazing. I know I don't deserve Your grace. Thank You for offering the gift of salvation to sinners. I confess I am a sinner and ask You to forgive my sins and wash me clean with the blood of my Jesus. Forgive me of all my sins and cleanse me of all my transgressions. I pray You will forgive my hidden faults, the sins I am not aware of, and help me avoid willful sin.

Holy Spirit, I declare I choose to forgive those who have sinned against me and I release them. Help me to forget all the wrongdoings that have been done against me so that they do not become strongholds in my life. I have confidence that You understand all about God's will and all about my life. I pray that each day You will show me how to bring those two together.

Lord Jesus, thank You for the strength You have given me to keep watching and praying so that I will not enter into temptation. I realize my spirit is willing but my flesh is often weak. Thank You for the sacrifice You made by giving Your life for me and for allowing me to be a part of the body of Christ. Thank You for showing me what true forgiveness looks like.

Father God, in reverence toward You and remembrance of Christ's death on the Cross and resurrection from the grave. I receive this bread, which represents the body of Christ, and this wine, which represents the blood of Christ.

Father God, I take this bread just as Jesus took a piece of bread and gave a prayer of thanks. Thank You for the body of Christ. In the breaking of this bread, I declare this piece of bread represents the broken body of Christ, which was given for me. When I eat this bread, I do it in remembrance of Jesus.

Father God, I take this cup just as Jesus took a cup and gave a prayer of thanks. Thank You for the blood of Christ. In lifting this cup I declare this cup represents the new covenant sealed with Jesus' blood, which is poured out for many for the forgiveness of sins. When I drink of this cup, I do so in remembrance of Jesus.

Heavenly Father, I pray that my life will demonstrate the depth of my commitment to live for the one who died for me. I lift high the Cross of Christ and proclaim Your great love. I have faith that Jesus' blood and broken body was all for love, and by taking communion, I am healed and restored. I am united in a fellowship with Jesus in the fullness of life.

In the precious name of Jesus I pray. Amen.

"Then Jesus took bread and spoke a prayer of thanksgiving. He broke the bread, gave it to them, and said, 'This is my body, which is given up for you. Do this to remember me." (Luke 22:19 GW)

Finding Shelter and Refuge

Lord Jesus, I declare that I dwell in the shelter of the Most High God. I rest in the shadow of the Almighty. I declare God is my refuge and my fortress, the only one in whom I completely trust. I will not wait until my world is falling apart to take refuge in the only real shelter and refuge I know; however, I will seek God day by day. I have faith I will find security in His promises.

Father God, I have confidence that You will save me from the fowler's snare and from the deadly pestilence. I have faith that You will cover me with Your protection and that under Your wings, I will find refuge. I am certain Your faithfulness will be my shield and guard around me. I confess I will not fear the terror of night or the arrows that fly by day or the diseases that stalk in the darkness or the plagues that destroy at midday.

Heavenly God, I declare that a thousand may fall at my side and ten thousand at my right hand but that no terror will come near me. I will only observe with my eyes and see the punishment of the wicked. I declare You are my refuge and my dwelling place. No harm will overtake me, and no disaster will come near my home. I have faith that You will command Your angels to guard me in all my ways. They will lift me up in their hands so that I will not strike my foot against a stone.

Lord Jesus, I have faith that with You, I will tread on the lion and the cobra. I will trample the great lion and the serpent. I am confident because I love You, You will rescue me and protect me. I acknowledge Your name, and I have faith that when I call on You, You will answer me. You will be with me in trouble, and You will deliver me and honor me with long life. You will satisfy me and show me my salvation.

In the precious name of Jesus I pray. Amen.

Rest in the shadow of the Almighty: (Psalm 91:1-16 KJV)

Blessed and Enlarged Territories

Heavenly Father, I desire to be used by You to expand Your kingdom here on earth. I pray that You will take and enlarge every good thing that You bring into my life. Please increase my family, friends, and relationships. I pray that You will give me opportunities and increase the influence and the impact that I have on others in such a manner that I will touch more lives for Your kingdom and for Your glory.

Father God, I pray You will assign me ministry positions and help me to speak Your Word with boldness, winning souls to Jesus with the Holy Spirit's guidance. Equip me with the resources and the skills I require so that I can bless Your kingdom. I declare I will put all that You give to me back into Your hands. I recognize that without You, I can do nothing right. I require Your strength to stand strong. I need Your power and presence with me always. I pray You will fill me with Your fullness, bless me, and help me prosper.

Father God, I pray that You will continually keep me from evil and from the temptation of sin. Deliver me from the Devil. I pray that You to place a supernatural barrier of safety around me. I believe that by Your power, I am safe. I pray that You will release a legion of Your angels to encamp around me and surround me with Your hedge of protection. I pray Your hand will be upon me in all that I do today and every day of my life.

Holy Spirit, help me to avoid making the same mistakes I so often make when temptation comes my way. I confess that I am a sinner and my choices are not always smart or in God's will. Deliver me from my spiritual bondages and emotional pain. Encourage me with my daily decisions, words, and actions. When I am weak, remind me that Jesus is my true source of love and happiness. Direct my steps away from all that is not of God and keep me far from evil. Keep me safe from the pain and the grief that my sins bring.

Lord Jesus, I pray You will help me watch and pray so that I will not fall into temptation. I realize that my spirit is ready but the body is weak. I recognize God is faithful and He will not allow me to be tempted beyond my ability, and I know it will take God's grace and His mighty hand to accomplish this in me. I am certain God is faithful to grant my request.

In the precious name of Jesus I pray. Amen.

"Jabez prayed to the God of Israel, 'Please bless me and give me more territory. May your power be with me and free me from evil so that I will not be in pain.' God gave him what he prayed for." (1 Chronicles 4:10 GW)

Breaking Free from Strongholds

Lord Jesus, I have faith that You intercede for me and You are always pleading my case before the Father. I declare You are the only mediator before the throne of the Almighty. I am certain that You alone have the power to mediate and intercede between God and man.

Gracious Heavenly Father, thank You for rescuing me. I could not live without You. I place my life in Your loving arms. I desire Your hand upon me all through my days. I believe Your Word, and I trust in Your promises. I have confidence that You promise to deliver me when I cry out to You for help. When I call upon Your name in the day of trouble, You will rescue me.

Father God, I ask You to free me from all ungodliness that is trying to place a stronghold on me. I believe that You will work deliverance in my life everywhere it is needed. I have confidence You have unshackled me from the power of darkness and empowered me for Your heavenly kingdom with the authority to overcome even the fiercest spiritual obstacles or strongholds of the Enemy.

Holy Spirit, I desire wisdom and revelation of what to pray for concerning strongholds. I pray that You let all that is hidden come to light. If there are any actions I need to take, show me and help me accomplish them. Please lead, guide, protect, cover, and strengthen me when sin is trying to take root. I pray that when evil is trying to place a stranglehold in my life, You will give me the wisdom, the courage, and the strength to stand and fight.

Lord Jesus, I declare that I might walk in the flesh but I do not war according to the flesh because the weapons I use in my battle are not made by humans. Rather, they are powerful weapons from God. With them, I can destroy every proud obstacle that sets itself up against the knowledge of God. I take captive every thought to make it obedient to God.

Father God, I declare I will run to You in times of troubles. You are my shield and my strength. My faith believes that You will unchain me from every evil thing and defend me from the Enemy. I know that in all things, You work for the good of those who love You, those who have been called according to Your purpose. I declare in all these things, I am more than a conqueror through Christ Jesus.

In the precious name of Jesus I pray. Amen.

"The weapons we use in our fight are not made by humans. Rather, they are powerful weapons from God. With them we destroy people's defenses, that is, their arguments and all their intellectual arrogance that oppose the knowledge of God. We take every thought captive so that it is obedient to Christ." (2 Corinthians 10:4-5 GW)

The Power of Positive Speaking

Father God, I believe that faith is the substance of things hoped for and the evidence of things not seen. I am confident You spoke and the universe was formed at Your command so that what is seen was made out of what was unseen.

Heavenly Father, I pray that You will give me the self-control to not let any unwholesome talk come out of my mouth. Only word that are helpful for building others up according to their needs. I pray that my words will benefit those who listen. I realize there is no such thing as idle words. Every one of my words counts, and by speaking positively, I will bring about healing, prosperity, joy, peace, and love. I have faith my positive words work for me, so I choose to fill my mouth with words of power that cannot be resisted. I declare my words bless and heal. They lead my loved ones into victory, and they charge the atmosphere of my home.

Father God, I believe in the power of words, and I am aware that by my words, I will be set free or condemned. I declare when I speak words in faith that line up with Your Word, I will have a positive result. On the other hand, if I speak words of doubt, I will eventually believe them and experience the negative things that those words produce.

Holy Spirit, I pray You will put a guard over my mouth, and keep watch over the door of my lips. I realize that my tongue has the power of life and death and what I speak is what I will get. I understand that my words can either be my most powerful weapon or they can become a hindrance. Help me to keep in mind that the words I speak will work for me or against me. Encourage me that those who guard their mouths and their tongues keep themselves from calamity, and that I can be trapped by what I say, and ensnared by the words of my mouth.

Father God, I believe that my faith is released by speaking Your Word over my situation. I have the authority to speak to the mountain, which can be any problem or situation I may be dealing with. I am certain that Jesus gave me the authority to speak to the problem itself. I believe that You have put certain things under my authority and I must exercise that authority.

Heavenly Father, In the name of Your one and only Son, Jesus Christ, my Lord and Savior, I demand that all spirits of negative words depart from me. I choose to speak words that produce life. I declare that I am positive, encouraging, optimistic, helpful, and cheerful and that my words bring harmony, reconciliation, and restoration.

Heavenly Father, I declare I am a winner. I am a champion, and I am the healed and whole. I walk with righteousness in Jesus Christ. In Him I live and move and have my being. I am certain when I believed in Christ, I became a new creation. The old way of living has disappeared, and a new way of living has come into existence. Since I am born-again, I am more than a conqueror, and I am a child of God. I reign in life as the King's kid, and I am seated in the heavenly realm, free from all condemnation.

In the precious name of Jesus I pray. Amen.

"Set a guard, O Lord, over my mouth; Keep watch over the door of my lips." (Psalm 141:3 NKJV)

The Keys of the Kingdom of Heaven

Lord Jesus, thank You for entrusting me with the keys to the kingdom of heaven. I take the authority I have been given in Your name with the power of the Holy Spirit in me. I claim dominion over all the earth and everything on it. I have faith that whatever I bind on earth will be bound in heaven and whatever I release on earth will be released in heaven.

Father God, I take my God-given authority, and I bind my will to Your will. I declare Your kingdom come and Your will be done in my life. I bind my feelings and emotions to the instruction of the Holy Spirit. I realize that my feelings are rarely very trustworthy; however, You alone know what is in store for me, so rather than trust my feelings, I put all my faith in You.

Father God, I bind my hands to the work that You have ordained and appointed for me. I declare I am happy in my work because it is a gift from You. I am certain every good and perfect gift is from above. I choose to have a purpose-driven life because You are the center of my life and Lord of my work.

Father God, I bind my feet to the path that You have placed before me so that I am in the right place at the right time. I declare in all my ways, I will acknowledge You. I have faith that You will make my paths straight. I declare Your Word is a lamp for my feet, a light on my path.

Father God, I bind my body to the plans and purpose that You placed within me. I declare that my body is a temple of the Holy Spirit. I praise You because I am fearfully and wonderfully made in Your Image. You created and knitted me together in my mother's womb.

Gracious Father, I bind my life to the truth that is in Your Word. I have chosen the way of truth, and I have set my heart on Your laws. I declare Jesus is the way, the truth, and the life. I will follow Your instructions, and I will always treasure Your commands. I choose to keep Your laws close to the pupil of my eye and bind them upon my fingers and write them upon the tablet of my heart.

Father God, I take authority as Your child and call my debts paid. I speak to my finances and tell them to come in line with Your Word. I believe that I am blessed with the promise of Abraham because I observe Your commandments. I am the head and not the tail. I am above and not beneath. I declare that You are my source and that recession, inflation, and every other economic downfall doesn't belong to me. I am Your child and a joint heir with Christ Jesus. I have confidence I am more than a conqueror, and I know that in all things, You work for the good of those who love You, those who have been called according to Your purpose.

Heavenly Father, In the name of Your one and only Son, Jesus Christ, my Lord and Savior. I banish the plans of the Enemy from my life. I forbid any counterfeit words, disease, rebellion, debt, un-forgiveness, or lack from my life. I reject all layers of complaints, uncertainty, or dishonesty that my soul has put in place. I combat anything that is not of Your will or that is displeasing to the Holy Spirit. I give the Holy Spirit reign over my life, my mind, my spirit, and my body.

In the precious name of Jesus I pray. Amen.

"I will give you the keys of the kingdom of heaven. Whatever you imprison, God will imprison. And whatever you set free, God will set free." (Matthew 16:19 GW)

Trusting God's Word

Father God, I have faith that all Scripture comes from Your breath and is useful for teaching, rebuking errors, correcting faults, and giving instruction for right ways of living. I declare that Your Word stands forever and that You will not alter the words that have gone out of Your mouth. Your Word is forever settled in heaven. I am confident that through Your words, I have received the grace to walk by faith and that I am rewarded for diligently seeking You.

Holy Spirit, remind me that my feelings can deceive. Help me to only accept as true what lines up with God's Word. I am certain the grass will wither, and the flowers will fade, but the word of God stands forever. I realize that in order to receive a miracle from God, one of the steps I must take is to trust God's Word completely and without hesitation. I have confidence God's ways are perfect and all the Lord's promises prove true.

Father God, I declare Jesus is a shield for all who look to Him for protection. My testimony is that Jesus is Lord of my life and I am Your child. I desire for Your will to de done in me and through me. I declare that I am blessed like faithful Abraham. I am a child of faith, born-again by Your incorruptible seed. I cherish that You made Jesus, who had no sin, bear my sin for me so that I might become righteous in Him.

Heavenly Father, I have faith that because I serve You, I am fully qualified and equipped to do every kind or good deed. I pray for the fullness of the ministry that You have appointed for me. I pray You will anoint me for all You have purposed to do through me. I pray You will call forth divine appointments and open doors of opportunity. I pray for God-ordained encounters and ministry positions that You have destined to accomplish through me before the foundation of this world.

Father God, I have faith that You are mindful of Your covenant with me. I trust in Your promises, and I receive these blessing by faith. I confess that I am healed and whole, that I have long life, that I am established, resilient, incorruptible, fruitful, productive, victorious, successful, full of peace, patient, bounding in gentleness, kind, meek, and full of self-control because I am filled with Your love.

In the precious name of Jesus I pray. Amen.

"Every Scripture passage is inspired by God. All of them are useful for teaching, pointing out errors, correcting people, and training them for a life that has God's approval. They equip God's servants so that they are completely prepared to do good things." (2 Timothy 3:16-17 GW)

Covered by the Blood of Jesus

Heavenly Father, I claim a hedge of protection by the application of the blood of Jesus around me, my husband, my children, and my family for a thousand generations. I declare no evil shall happen to Your righteous children and that the Devil cannot touch us.

Holy Spirit, I dispatch warrior angels to surround us, to protect our health, households, possessions, businesses, and finances from any harmful attack of the Enemy. I tear down any strongholds built within our minds that would alter our thinking process from operating in truth and love and cover the root of its origin with the blood of Jesus.

Father God, I declare that the blood of Jesus seals my words. I reckon my flesh dead on the Cross and my spirit alive unto You. I cast down every vain imagination that exalts itself above or in place of Jesus and the pattern of His holiness as set forth in the Holy Scripture. I declare that they shall never spring forth again.

Gracious God, according to Your blood covenant, I have the confidence to approach Your throne through the blood of Jesus, which was shed for me on the Cross at Calvary. I have faith that Jesus' blood serves as the sacrifice for all my sins, allowing me to cultivate a relationship with You. I declare that as Your child, I am like a tree that thrives because I am fed continually by the Holy Spirit, like an olive tree flourishing in the house of God.

Father God, in the name of Jesus Christ, I take my God-given authority over Satan and declare that he has no right or authority over my life, my husband, my children, my family, our homes, our minds, our health, our finances, our property, our possessions, our wealth, our business, or anything that we have authority over. I terminate all of the Enemy's evil assignments against us this day and render powerless all the efforts to harm us. I proclaim this by the authority given to me through my blood covenant with my Lord and Savior, Jesus Christ.

Holy Spirit, I invite You to infuse the spaces in us that I have removed by this prayer, with the mind of Christ, the fruit of the Spirit love, joy, peace, patience, kindness goodness, and faithfulness, and the passion of God. I declare we are hidden with Christ, the Anointed One, and I trust in God's unfailing love forever and ever.

In the precious name of Jesus I pray. Amen.

"But I am like a large olive tree in God's house. I trust the mercy of God forever and ever." (Psalm 52:8 GW)

Taking Authority with My Words

Heavenly Father, I place on the whole armor of God, and I take my God-given spiritual authority over this day, the Devil, all his demons, and all those people who are influenced by them. I declare by my faith, and my words, and the authority given to me by Jesus that I have power, and victory over the power of the Enemy. For that reason, he is under my feet and shall remain there by the works of the Cross of Calvary.

Father God, I take the authority that Jesus has given me, and I speak to my adversaries. I imprison all spirits of division, conflict, and wrath. I fill those empty spaces with unity, peace, and serenity. I imprison all spirits of criticism, gossip, and insult. I fill those empty spaces with praise, truth, and kind word. I imprison all spirits of guilt, arrogance, resentment. I fill those empty spaces with innocence, humility, forgiveness. I imprison all spirits of difficulty, delay, deception. I fill those empty spaces with ease, readiness, and truthfulness.

Father God, I imprison all spirits of deficiency, unfairness, retaliation. I fill those empty spaces with surplus, fairness and forgiveness. I imprison all spirits of confusion, distress. I fill those empty spaces with clarity and harmony. I imprison all spirits of the occults, witchcraft, idolatry, whether named or unnamed, know or unknown, from myself, my family, my loved ones, my household, my ministry, my daily purpose, my finances, and all people and all things for which I am responsible for or have ownership over. I fill those empty spaces with Jesus, Your Word, and the Holy Spirit.

Gracious Father, I imprison all curses that have ever been spoken against my life, my family, my loved ones, and my finances, and I dispel all curses that are the result of mine or my ancestors' behavior, words, actions, or practices from affecting our lives for a thousand generations. I imprison the power of negative speaking from others. I render useless all prayers intentionally (or unintentionally) not inspired by the Holy Spirit.

Father God, I ask for forgiveness for all the judgments that I have made against others. I release the judgments that have been made against me, and I forgive those who made them. I declare that I will treat my enemies with grace. I will bless those who curse me. I pray blessings on all who mistreat, insult, curse, or desire to do harm to me. I bless all enemies who hold grudges toward me personally, my family, my loved ones, my household, my finances, my church, my ministry, and my nation.

Father God, I declare that I am Your child and I am totally submitted to You. I have the power to resist the Devil and the authority to defeat him. I confess that no weapon formed against me shall prosper because You are my strength and shield. I renounce evil spirits, strongholds, false beliefs, and worldly thinking. In place of those things, I invite the Holy Spirit to abide in me with Your truth, Your love, and Your Word. I declare that I will walk in Your love and I will follow Your steps and I will not follow any other voice.

Holy Spirit, open my eyes to see the truth in every situation. Lead and guide me every day of my life. Help me distinguish between the righteous and the wicked. Help me avoid living by my own strength or by my own flesh. Encourage me to speak the gospel faithfully, to obey God always, to impart grace freely, and count on my Heavenly Father for everything.

In the precious name of Jesus I pray. Amen.

"Christ has redeemed us from the curse of the law, having become a curse for us, for it is written, cursed is everyone who hangs on a tree." (Galatians 3:13 NKJV)

Developing Godly Self-Esteem

Gracious Father God, I pray You will give me confidence and high self-esteem but also teach me to be humble. Help me to clothe myself in humility by reminding me of who I am in Christ. When I am feeling less than what You created me to be, confirm that You formed me in the womb, and You knew me before I was born, and You set me apart. I pray You will open my eyes to see an accurate view of myself by understanding Your view of who I am.

Holy Spirit, help me to remember that Jesus thought I was so precious that He poured out His life for every wrong thing I have ever done. Strengthen me to see that it is my inner beauty, and my gentle and quiet spirit, that is of great worth in God's sight. That life is about whom I am becoming and that all my abilities, experiences, battles, and weaknesses, compose a divine tapestry to bring out who God created me to be so that I can accomplish all that He has put me here to do.

Father God, I pray that You deliver me from all the lies that the Devil has placed against me. I release all the curses that have been made against me. I pray that You eliminate all doubt and unworthiness from my mind. Heal me of any pain or heartaches from my past that are affecting my future and my self-esteem. Help me feel loved and accepted first by You and then by others.

Holy Spirit, I recognize my self-esteem is connected to the way I judge my own worth. Help me to see myself as God sees me, and accept His bottomless, affectionate, and unchanging love. Help me to remember that my happiness depends entirely on me continuing in the love of Christ. I realize I have no source of permanent joy apart from that love. Teach me to abide in the love of Jesus. Help me recognize how much my real worth comes from being close to the one, who gave me my worth.

Heavenly Father, fill my heart with Your endless love. I pray I will I feel it penetrate my heart and spirit. I declare that I am blessed with the awesome gifts that You give so freely. I pray You will reveal to me Your loving kindness in the morning and Your soft whisper in the evening. I declare that I will trust in You at all times. Help me always remember that You love me so much that You sent Your one and only Son to die for me.

In the precious name of Jesus I pray. Amen.

"You should clothe yourselves instead with the beauty that comes from within, the unfading beauty of a gentle and quiet spirit, which is so precious to God." (1 Peter 3:4 NLT)

Speaking Only Words of Life

Heavenly Father, I declare I choose to speak life, healing, and restoration over myself and those I love. I pray You will train me to speak only words of life. Take control of my conversations and let them be full of grace and seasoned with salt so that I may know how to answer everyone. I know the tongue can bring death or life; and those who love to talk will reap the consequences. I believe that my words are like a sword I use in battle for success and happiness, and what I say and how I say it makes a huge difference. I am certain the words of the reckless pierce like a sharp edge but the tongue of the wise brings healing.

Holy Spirit, please give me spiritual ears to hear before I say something that is hurtful. I know that angry, reckless, or critical words are weapons and that they are so easy to speak. I need Your help daily so I will not speak wounding words. I realize that once I speak them, there is no way to get my words back, and long after I have forgotten them, someone else might still be feeling the hurt, by hearing my words over and over again. I recognize that my words take a moment but that the wounds can last for years.

Father God, I have confidence that the tongue of the wise brings healing and there is tremendous power in kind and gentle words. The simplest word of encouragement or support can brighten somebody's day. This is the kind of speech that I desire to be on my lips. I pray You will give me the wisdom to speak healing words. I believe that life-giving power lies in my speech, and I have the power to build up and impart grace, to speak truth and bring freedom, to encourage and support, to praise and thank, to express love and joy.

Heavenly Father, please help me hold my tongue. Stop my negative words before they come out of my mouth. Help me to speak what is true, noble, just, pure, lovely, good, virtuous, and praiseworthy. If my words are not these things, don't let them exit my mouth. Give me the encouraging gift of mindful and well-thought-out speech. I pray my words will reveal my heart and my mouth will only speak wisdom, truth, peace, love, and hope.

In the precious name of Jesus I pray. Amen.

"The tongue can bring death or life; those who love to talk will reap the consequences." (Proverbs 18:21 NIV)

Becoming a Virtuous Woman in the Eyes of God

Father God, thank You for all the blessings You have given me. I am so grateful that I am Your daughter, an heir with Jesus. I am certain that my righteousness comes through my faith in Jesus. Therefore, I have the right to come boldly before Your throne and receive answers to my prayers.

Heavenly Father, I trust and speak Your Word over all areas of my life. I desire the sincere milk of Your Word so that I can grow in the things that please You. I yearn for Your perfect will for my life, and I will walk in a manner that is worthy of Your blessings. I choose to reflect on the great things You have done for me, as I renew my mind in the Word daily, taking on the mind of Christ. I understand that apart from Jesus, I can do nothing.

Holy Spirit, encourage me to live in such a way that the gifts of wisdom, faith, knowledge, discernment, healing, miracles, prophecy, the gifts of tongue, and the gifts of interpretation will be manifest in my life. I confess that I am a gifted and hard-working woman with honest qualities and strength. I request to have God's favor on my life more than that of man. For that reason I will not conform to this world but will be transformed by the renewing of my mind.

Father God, I respect You therefore, I choose to dress appropriately. I take good care of my body at all times because my body is the Holy Spirit's temple. I take excellent care of myself so that I am able to care for my family. I declare I am successful in every good work. I manage my household with godly wisdom. I choose to keep Your commands and abide in Your love as a result my house is overflowing with Your love.

Father God, I choose to present myself to You as a living sacrifice, fully, and completely without reservation, and holding nothing back. I believe You treasure this kind of worship. I pray You will help me prosper in all things and bless me with good health as my soul prospers. I proclaim that my mind is sharp, my eyesight is clear; my healthy is excellent, my body is physically fit, and my comprehension is strong. There is nothing missing or broken in me.

Gracious Heavenly Father, I declare that I am empowered with wisdom to resolve challenges because You give me ideas, concepts, and inventions. I proclaim that I have the power to obtain wealth and I have more than enough. I handle my money wisely because I seek Your wisdom. I do not waste precious time sitting around idle. I take care of all my duties in a timely and efficient manner.

In the precious name of Jesus I pray. Amen.

"Fear the Lord, and serve him sincerely. Consider the great things he did for you." (1 Samuel 12:24 GW)

Healed from the Inside Out

Dear Heavenly Father, I praise Your Holy name because You are God Almighty, the King of kings and the Lord of lords. I declare Your mercy, love, and grace endure forever. You are my refuge and my hiding place in times of trouble. I have confidence that You care for those who trust in You. You will protect me from trouble and surround me with songs of deliverance. When I wait upon You, I will renew my strength, I will run, and not be weary, and I will walk, and not be faint.

Father God, I declare I will not worry about anything, but in every situation, I will let You know what I need in prayer while I give thanks. Thank You for all the prayers that You have already answered, the ones I can see and the ones You have not yet revealed to me. I am certain if I wait patiently, You will turn to me and hear my prayers. I believe when I ask for anything that is according to Your will, I shall receive them. I have faith that before I call, You answer and while I am still speaking, You hear my cry. You know what is best for me and Your timing is prefect.

Father God, I pray You will heal me from the inside out. I declare that my body is healthy and strong. My faith in You assures me of the things I expect and convinces me of the things I cannot see. I have faith that You are the healer of the brokenhearted, the one who bandages my wounds. I am certain You give me power when I am weak, and when I have no might, You increase my strength. I am confident when I call to You for help, You heal me. You bring health to my body and nourishment to my bones.

Gracious Father, thank You for the spiritual weapons of warfare You have given me. I declare that the authority of Jesus is far greater than the power of darkness, so the Enemy must yield. The yoke of sickness, pain, lack, and just getting by are destroyed. I pray You will rebuke the Devourer for my namesake and You will bind Satan from my life. I pray that all strongholds and curses that have been made against me will stop affecting my life, my health, my well-being, and my Christian walk, and that they will never restructure again.

Holy Spirit, I receive a supernatural healing that can only come from God by the precious blood of Jesus. I declare that Jesus bore the stripes on His back for my sins and that by His stripes, I am healed. I have faith that through the sacrifice made on the Cross of Calvary, all my sins are forgiven and all my diseases are healed. I am grateful for my legions of warring angels that encamp all-around me and the hedge of divine protection that covers me.

In the precious name of Jesus I pray. Amen.

"Then Jesus took bread and spoke a prayer of thanksgiving. He broke the bread, gave it to them, and said, 'This is my body, which is given up for you. Do this to remember me." (Luke 22:19 GW)

Caring for the Holy Spirit's Temple

Heavenly Father, I surrender myself to You. I realize that this is not my body to do with what I please. I acknowledge that I do not have the right to drink what I want, eat what I want, watch what I want, or listen to what I want. I confess that my body is the Holy Spirit's temple. I realize that with everything I do, no matter how small or routine, I should consider what my behavior says about my faith.

Father God, I have faith that Jesus came to mend broken hearts and set the captives free, which He is still doing today. I proclaim that Jesus has set me free, so I have freedom from overeating, emotional eating, and fad diets. I have confidence I am healed and whole. I declare as I grow older, the light of Jesus will continue to shine through me because I take care of the Holy Spirit's temple. I pray my radiant skin will reflect that light, and will I become physically stronger and healthier every day.

Holy Spirit, encourage me to eat healthy. Let me be dissatisfied by foods that are not good for my body. I declare that with every action that I take, even eating and drinking, I will keep in mind that my body is not my own. I confess I have the desire and willpower to treat my body well. I pray that the food I crave will bring nourishment and I will have no desire for unhealthy food. I pray for the self-discipline to exercise daily and eat fresh fruits, vegetable, lean meats, fish, and healthy grains, and drink plenty of water to hydrate my body.

Father God, I acknowledge that You designed and created my body and You created food for both nutrition and enjoyment. I confess what I eat or drink, I do it all for Your glory. I declare that because I eat well, I have the energy to complete all that I need to do. Therefore, I do not sit around sluggish but I use my energy to serve You and others.

In the precious name of Jesus I pray. Amen.

"Don't you know that you are God's temple and that God's Spirit lives in you? If anyone destroys God's temple, God will destroy him because God's temple is holy. You are that holy temple." (1 Corinthians 3:16-17 GW)

The Gift of Eternal Life

Father God, my words cannot describe how grateful I am for the tremendous gifts I have received from You. Thank You for calling me Your own and giving me eternal life in Christ Jesus. Your love is so amazing and Your mercy is all that I have ever needed. I don't know where I would be if not for Your grace. I realize I was living a life so far from Your will, yet You reached for me. While my life was full of sin and rebellion, You called my name. While I was broken and empty, You mended my heart and filled my spirit. You filled my heart with great joy and absolute peace by giving me the gift of eternal life.

Father God, I believe that the wages of sin is death but the gift of eternal life through Christ Jesus, is from You. That is why I surrender completely to You. I desire to develop my personal relationship with You more than anything. I want to overflow with Your Word, be led by the Holy Spirit, and nearby You always.

Heavenly Father, I give You my mind. Saturate it with Your wisdom. I give You my hands. Assign me work in Your kingdom. I give You my feet. Guide me down the path You have planned for me. I give You my eyes. Show me Your will for my life. I give You my ears. Tell me Your plans. I give You my mouth. Speak through me with boldness, spreading the gospel of peace. I give You my heart. The unconditional love that You have given me so freely is what I desire to offer and shower on others.

Holy Spirit, I give You permission to make me more like Jesus. Progressively free me from my sinful habits and transform me into the likeness of Christ. Empower me to replace ungodly habits with godly fruits like love, patience, and self-control. Encourage me to live in such a way that the gifts of the spirit like wisdom, knowledge, discernment, faith, healing, miracles, and prophecy, the gifts of tongues, and the gifts of the interpretation will be manifest in my life. Change me in such a way that others will see the gift of eternal life ever-increasingly in me.

In the precious name of Jesus I pray. Amen.

"For the wages of sin is death, but the gift of God is eternal life in Christ Jesus our Lord." (Romans 6:23 NKJV)

Giving Thanks at All Times

Gracious Heavenly Father, I am grateful for the gift of salvation. Thank You for grace and mercy. I am thankful I do not need to worry about anything, but in all situations, I will call on You in prayer while I give thanks. I proclaim I will enter Your gates with thanksgiving and I will go into Your courtyards with praise. I proclaim You are my Father and I am so grateful to be Your child. I declare that my life is hidden in Christ and I no longer live but Christ lives through me.

Lord Jesus, You make it possible for me to maintain a spirit of praise and thankfulness, even in the most trying circumstances. I feel Your grace extended to me. I have victory over sin and death, and that victory is achieved through You. I am certain that my spiritual weapons are mighty for the pulling down of strongholds. However I ask You too help me watch and pray so that I will not fall into temptation. I realize my spirit is willing but the body is weak.

Holy Spirit, encourage me to pray without ceasing and to give thanks in all circumstances. I believe this is God's will for me in Christ Jesus. I have faith that God works all things together for the good of those who love Him. I desire to develop an appreciative spirit, giving thanks for the good things in life and looking for ways in which God bring blessings out of even the most difficult situations. I have decided to praise God in the good times and the bad.

Heavenly Father, I acknowledge that there are many things that could determine my attitude and my words. I pray You will teach me to become humble and thankful for everything. I pray the peace of the Holy Spirit will take root in my heart even in the most frustrating circumstances. I have faith that Your peace surpasses all understanding. I believe that being humble and thankful are very important qualities for me to exhibit. I realize that thankfulness is a key part of my Christian walk.

Gracious Heavenly Father, thank You for my family, my friends, my church, my ministries, my possessions, my businesses, and my finances. Thank You for making me a steward over all You have placed in my hands. Thank You for the opportunities that You give me every day. I pray You will help me make wise choices and give me the courage to do Your will.

In the precious name of Jesus I pray. Amen.

"Whatever happens, give thanks, because it is God's will in Christ Jesus that you do this." (1 Thessalonians 5:18 GW)

Maintaining the Joy of the Lord

Father God, I realize that true joy and happiness is in Your presence. I choose too wake up every morning mindful that this is the day that You have made, and I choose too rejoice and be glad in it. I will continually depend on the vast treasure I have in You and Your promises so that I will experience Your abundant, overflowing joy. I declare I am filled with the joy of the Holy Spirit and Your joy rises up in my soul. I pray You have set me above by anointing me with the oil of joy.

Father God, I realize that joy is a gift from You that enables me to find hope and peace even when life seems to be falling apart. I pray that even in the ups and downs of life, the joy of the Holy Spirit will give me strength to endure. I have faith that You understand everything that I face and You promise to provide for all my needs. I am certain Your joy will carry me through even the deepest pain. I proclaim that Your love is unconditional and You will never abandon me.

Father God, I realize there are so many things that seek to rob me of joy. Sometimes my circumstances can shake my faith. People will discourage me. Things will distract me from what You want me to enjoy. I also understand that joy is an attitude I choose to express. I declare my joy comes from the Holy Spirit dwelling in me and my confidence in You. I believe that You are at work and fully in control of whatever is happening, or will ever happen. I declare my joy does not depend on my circumstances because my joy rests in Your sovereign control of all things.

Lord Jesus, I realized that I could only come to God from where I am. I am certain when I stood before You with my life in shambles, mourning over my sins, I heard You whisper to me. For that reason, I will not grieve, for the joy of the Lord is my strength. I declare that weeping may remain for a night but that rejoicing comes in the morning. Thank You for the joy of the Holy Spirit. I am certain I am in Your glorious presence without fault and with great joy, and I am filled with an indescribable and glorious joy.

Holy Spirit, refresh my heart with God's love, which provides me great happiness and overflowing encouragement so that my joy may be complete. I have faith that a deep and abiding rejoicing is promised to those who abide in Christ and obey God's commandments. I find joy in knowing that whomever the Son sets free is free indeed. I speak joy, peace, comfort, and love over my life. I choose to rejoice in my salvation, and I have faith that Your truth has set me free.

Father God, Jesus told us to ask for anything in His name, so I have faith that when I ask, I will receive. In Jesus' name, I break the power of any negative emotions that are surrounding me and stealing my joy.

I proclaim that negative and ungodly attitudes have no place in my mind. I have confidence when they come, the Holy Spirit will comfort me and give me the peace that surpasses all understanding. I declare that the Holy Spirit is able to keep me from stumbling because I love righteousness and hate wickedness.

In the precious name of Jesus I pray. Amen.

"So far you haven't asked for anything in my name. Ask and you will receive so that you can be completely happy." (John 16:24 GW)

When God's People Pray

Father God, I am convinced when I pray, Your glory comes. You come to rule, to reign, and to show Your authority. I am certain You come to show that the government is upon Your shoulder, not upon anyone else's.

Gracious Heavenly Father, I cry out for this nation and for the nation of Israel. I pray that You will hear my prayers as I humble myself in prayer and seek Your face. I pray that the people of this nation and the nation of Israel will turn from their selfish ways and seek You with all their hearts. I have faith that You will hear from heaven, forgive our sins, and make our land prosperous again.

Father God, open the eyes of this lost and rebellious generation. Call their name and draw them close to You. I pray that the people of this nation and the nation of Israel will open their eyes and see the truth. I pray that they will humble themselves before You and repent of their sins. I pray they will understand how You will change lives when we set aside our own agendas and take You at Your Word and listen for Your voice.

Holy Spirit, reveal the truth to this generation and bring them to their salvation. Bring to light the truth that Jesus died in their place and came to save and rescue them from their spiritual death penalty. Reveal to the world that no one comes to the Father except through Jesus. I pray that the world will come to understand that the peace that they are searching for, the forgiveness of sins and the healing of our countries will only come when we get on our knees and seek God's face.

In the precious name of Jesus I pray. Amen.

"However, if my people, who are called by my name, will humble themselves, pray, search for me, and turn from their evil ways, then I will hear their prayer from heaven, forgive their sins, and heal their country." (2 Chronicles 7:14 GW)

Fresh Anointing

Gracious Heavenly Father, I am grateful for access to the Holy Spirit's fresh anointing. I desire Your presence and power in my life. I am certain that You do not call the equipped but You equip the called. I pray for Your burden-removing, yoke-destroying, anointing power over my life. I am confident the yoke of the Devil is destroyed because of the anointing. I am grateful that the anointing oil represents the anointing of the Holy Spirit. I have faith for a fresh anointing of joy, healing, and restoration in my life.

Father God, as an act of consecration and dedication to You, I anoint myself with oil. I offer my body to You as a living sacrifice. I view my being anointed with oil as a physical manifestation of being filled continuously with the Holy Spirit.

Father God, I anoint my mind. I declare that I will not be conformed to this world but that I will be transformed by the renewing of my mind. I pray that You will change the way I think so that all I do will line up with Your Word. It is my desire to understand, comprehend and discern Your Word.

Father God, I anoint my eyes. I declare that I will keep my eyes on Jesus, the foundation and finisher of my faith. I pray You will open my eyes to see the truth of Your Holy Scripture, the needs of others around me, and the beauty of the things that You have made. I pray my eyes will be open to see the blessings You have placed in front of me. It is my desire to clearly see everything You have planned for me.

Father God, I anoint my ears to listen for Your whisper. I pray You will open my ears so that I can hear You speak. It is my desire to recognize Your voice when I hear it in whatever way that You choose to communicate with me.

Father God, I anoint my mouth. I pray that the words of my mouth and the meditation of my heart are acceptable in Your sight. I pray that my words will encourage, support, and build up those around me. It is my desire for my words to speak life and healing.

Father God, I anoint my heart. I will honor and serve You with acts of kindness that come from my heart. I declare that my heart is the spiritual core of my being and the life force of my spiritual nature. Every heartbeat is a gift from You, and my heart is where You meet me, where You nudge me to change and guide my life. It is my desire to delight myself in You. I am certain that You will give me the desires of my heart.

Father God, I anoint my hands. I trust that I will have the victory in all battles over my enemies when I keep my hands raised in praise to You. I pray that the works of my hands will give You glory because my work is Your gift to me. It is my desire for You to establish the works of my hands.

Father God, I anoint my feet. I declare that Your Word is a lamp unto my feet and a light unto my path. I pray You will lead me down the path that You have ordained for me. It is my desire to go about doing good deeds for Your kingdom's cause, walking in integrity with full assurance that I am walking in the steps You have ordered for me.

In the precious name of Jesus I pray. Amen.

"It shall come to pass in that day, that his burden will be taken away from your shoulder and his yoke from your neck and the yoke will be destroyed because of the anointing oil." (Isaiah 10:27 NKJV)

Reasons to Believe

Heavenly Father, I believe that You are the one and only true living God. I believe that I received salvation through the confession of Jesus Christ as my Lord and Savior. I believe that salvation is found in no one else and there is no other name under heaven given to mankind by which we can be saved. I believe that there are three persons in the Godhead the Father, the Son, and the Holy Spirit. I believe all Scripture is God-breathed and that it is useful for teaching, rebuking, correcting, and training in righteousness.

Father God, I have faith that Jesus Christ is the true Emmanuel. He was conceived in the Virgin Mary by the Holy Spirit. He is Your only begotten Son. I believe Jesus was crucified, buried, and rose from the dead. He ascended into heaven and today, He is at Your right hand as our intercessor. I have faith when I repented of my sins and trusted in Jesus Christ, I was justified and declared righteous under the blood of Jesus.

Father God, I believe in the baptism of the Holy Spirit and the speaking in other tongues as the Holy Spirit gives the utterance as the initial evidence of this experience. I believe in the nine gifts of the Holy Spirit, including wisdom, knowledge, discernment, faith, healing, miracles, and prophecy, the gifts of tongue, and the gifts of interpretation. I pray I will live so that these gifts may be manifest in my life.

Father God, I believe You have given me the freedom to worship. I desire that my every form of expression is done in integrity and order, showing respect and honor to You so as not to draw attention to myself. I declare that I will follow the anointing of the Holy Spirit as I offer my body as a living sacrifice, holy and pleasing to You. I believe this is my spiritual act of worship.

Father God, I believe that it is Your will for every believer to be baptized by immersion in water in the name of the Father, the Son, and the Holy Spirit. I believe it is an act of obedience symbolizing the believer's faith in a crucified, buried, and risen Savior. It symbolizes the believer's death to sin, the burial of the old life, and the resurrection to walk in spotlessness with Christ Jesus.

Father God, I believe that Jesus' body was broken for my healing and He has delivered me from the power of disease. I am so grateful that You are my great physician. I am thankful for Your divine healing for my body. I believe that sometimes You heal us by Your touch or Your Word and at other times You work through doctors.

Father God, I believe the atonement of Jesus Christ was an indispensable part of Your plan for Your Son's earthly mission and our salvation. There is no greater expression of love than the gracious atonement Jesus courageously fulfilled. I believe that every blessing I receive from You comes through the merits of the atonement sacrificed for us on Calvary. I wait patiently for the second coming of my Lord and Savior, Jesus Christ. I pray for the salvation of my friends and family. I believe that those who die outside of Christ will be punished in an eternal hell but those who die in Him shall share in His glory in heaven forever.

Father God, I believe the sacredness of marriage between one man and one woman is Your will. I pray that this nation's eyes will be opened to see marriage through Your eyes. I believe that abortion is killing human life. I pray that the people of this nation will understand that You saw our unformed bodies and all our days are written in Your book before one of them occurs. I pray the world will acknowledge that You treasure all life and strong family values.

In the precious name of Jesus I pray. Amen.

"Let it be known to you therefore, brothers, that through this man forgiveness of sins is proclaimed to you." (Acts 13:38 ESV)

CPSIA information can be obtained at www.ICGtesting.com
Printed in the USA
LVOW07s1213011113

359551LV00001B/1/P